when blackness rhymes

when blackness rhymes with blackness

ROWAN RICARDO PHILLIPS

Dalkey Archive Press
Champaign and London

Earlier versions of these essays appeared in *A Companion to African-American Studies, A Concise Companion to Twentieth-century American Poetry*, *Small Axe*, and the *Kenyon Review*

Library of Congress Cataloging-in-Publication Data

Phillips, Rowan Ricardo.
 When blackness rhymes with blackness / Rowan Ricardo Phillips. -- 1st ed.
   p. cm.
 ISBN 978-1-56478-583-1 (pbk. : acid-free paper)
 1. American poetry--African American authors--History and criticism. I. Title.
 PS310.N4P47 2010
 811.009'896073--dc22
                    2010012095

Partially funded by the University of Illinois at Urbana-Champaign and by a grant from the Illinois Arts Council, a state agency

The author would like to thank Stony Brook University for its generous support of this project

www.dalkeyarchive.com

for my parents

CONTENTS

What happens when blackness rhymes with blackness? In other words, what happens to our sense of the poetic experience when we read an African-American poem?

How do we know an African-American poem is an African-American poem when we read one? Of course, we don't. We fashion our desire to think of African-American poetry as African-American poetry, and in some sense that proves to be sufficient. Yet what we recognize when we think we recognize an African-American poem is either the race of the author ("I know this poet is black"), the context of the poem ("I am reading this poem in an anthology of African-American poetry"), or some form of self-referential content ("Yet do I marvel at this curious thing: / To make a poet black, and bid him sing!"). There is no such thing a priori as an African-American poem. And not only is there nothing wrong with that, but acknowledging this would make our considerations of African-American poetry stronger for it.

This collection of essays is concerned first and foremost with understanding the moods by which what we call African-American poetry works within and without towards and against an allegorical sense of itself: Phillis Wheatley as an allegory and epigraph to the larger, prosaic impetus of the African-American literary tradition; Frederick Douglass's poetic dilemma and its impact on his prose; the blues and jazz as antagonists to the poet instead of a platform from which the poet "gives voice" to the musician; Derek Walcott's use of meter and landscape as the unexpected counterpoint to the overdetermined phenomenological experience of Caribbeanness; and, finally, a verse essay in ten-word terza rima (the word, as it is the basic unit of an essay, replacing the syllable as the basic unit of the essay in verse) on Robert Hayden's use of the ballad. The objective of these essays is to re-situate a number of poetic conversations I have found overburdened by an allegorical sense of what happens or should happen when blackness rhymes with blackness.

Take Robert Hayden's "Ballad of Nat Turner," the note upon which this book ends. The ballad is written in the voice of Nat Turner instead of that of an anonymous narrator, which is the traditional tendency of the genre of the ballad. Moved to describe the decisive moment of his life that led to this poem, Turner says that

> The spirits vanished. Afraid and lonely
> I wandered on in blackness.
> Speak to me now or let me die.
> Die, whispered the blackness.[1]

---

1 Robert Hayden, "The Ballad of Nat Turner," *Collected Poems*, ed. Frederick Glaysher (New York: Liveright, 1985), 56–58.

Does "blackness" rhyme with "blackness" here? Are they two separate words, or a mere repetition of the same phenomena? They are different. One blackness is spatial, it is wandered through; the other is a speaking subject. Its speech act is paradoxical: a didactic whisper. Turner, here as the poet, has asked blackness to bestow onto him one out of two options: to speak to him *or* to let him die. But what blackness does is speak to him . . . *and* tell him to die. Blackness changes the speaker's "or" to "and" and offers itself as both prized equality and terrifying annihilation. In other words, blackness speaks (which is Turner's wish, after all) but in speaking disregards the contingent nature of the speaker's speech act and wish. As a conjunction, "or" is the sign of alternatives, substitutes, and opinions of supposedly equal importance. Yet without further elaboration, "or" also simultaneously offers exclusion ("speak or let me die, *but not both*") and possibility ("speak or let me die, *possibly both*"); outside of the speech act, we are left to choose one, or to decide not to decide. The English language is such that when we form a sentence as merely "b or c" ("speak to me now or let me die"), and that is all we know, we then have no privileged knowledge of whether "or" intends to be inclusive or exclusive. The moment has an embedded, problematic quality to it in regards to the manner in which allegorical utterance of blackness destabilizes the voice formed by poems. And within this moment, this benign turned on a benign word, "The Ballad of Nat Turner" reveals an archetypal conflict within the greater narrative archetypal conflict—namely the role of blackness in determining both seen and unseen outcomes of poetic encounter with the imagination and its ineffable counterpart, ineffable blackness itself.

A proposition and poignantly ironic character within the poem writ large, the value of what blackness then can say exists independent of the poet who conceives of the statement as an exclusive disjunction of two propositions, for blackness responds with an inclusive disjunction. Blackness enters our poems as an other, speaking, making with our language something to be better understood. And whether it is to be understood as something new or as simply the same old voice, whether it is the sounds of a new rhyme or just mere repetition is in the balance for us to decide. This is what happens, and is the challenge to us, when blackness rhymes with blackness.

She was a shadow as thin in memory
As an autumn ancient underneath the snow,
Which one recalls at a concert or in a café.

Phillis Wheatley would be African-American literature's first idea, but she is its epigraph. Although Lucy Terry, Francis Williams, and Jupiter Hammon all preceded her, an insistent clamor of firstness has accompanied Phillis Wheatley with nearly every evocation of her name. Born somewhere in West Africa, sometime around 1753—slavery has blotted out the specifics—she was brought to America in a metaphor: stowed in the hold of a slaver named *Phillis*, her Christian name presaging her in its dark wet wood. Purchased on the 11th of June 1761 in Boston by the Wheatley family, she settled in (if that's the word for it) as a domestic servant in the house on the corner of what are now State and Kilby streets.

By all accounts, she was a precocious child. John Wheatley, in a letter that would form part of the preface of her book of poems, wrote that in sixteen months she "attained the English Language, to which she was an utter Stranger before, to such a Degree, as to read any, the most difficult Parts of the Sacred Writings." She swept through English and moved on to Latin, by twelve she was writing poetry—"her own curiosity led her to it," John Wheatley confessed.

Her first published poem, an elegy for a clergyman, appeared in *The Newport Mercury* in December 1767. And throughout her life her poetry would be steered primarily toward happenings: she composed public addresses, elegies, panegyrics, hymns. She possessed a near perfect pitch when it came to pitting poem to circumstance; she wrote about the right people and with the right tone—dignitaries, the famous dead, grand public figures, and sympathy-inducing grievers . . . soon she was in vogue on both sides of the Atlantic. Poems in London papers popped up. In France, she was on the tips of the lips of the literati. She began to collect her poems into a book. She was barely twenty.

Eventually, the inability to find a publisher in America led Phillis and her mistress, Susannah Wheatley, to London where she sought and won the patronage of the Countess of Huntingdon. It was there that *Poems on Various Subjects, Religious and Moral* was first published, going for sale on the 11th of September 1773. John Wheatley's aforementioned letter would form part of the preface, along with an attestation to the veracity and merits of the author that was signed by eighteen of Boston's most renowned men, including the governor, the lieutenant governor, John Hancock, and John Wheatley himself, who was noted as "her master." It would be the only book Phillis Wheatley would ever publish.

She wrote in rhymed couplets and composed almost exclusively in iambic pentameter. Aside from a few letters, the tempo of that meter is the only music by which we know her thoughts. Evangelical neoclassicism is the root chord of her poems. Pope in technique and Gray in theme tend to lend to her lines a ring more English than American, although in her day that was a fairly thin line to cross. The barely hidden hints of Horace in her work are as unmistakable as her use of Roman mythology was unremarkable. She was, in this sense, a real poet of the eighteenth century, when poetry was practically synonymous with frill and code. How far toward a rebellious African heart that code may have swung we will never know. Some pin all hope they have of Phillis Wheatley on this, others on her characterization as the inaugural poet, regardless of how spurious that claim may be. To read her poems in search of a cause instead causes a slight feeling of guilt—you feel you're missing something—you read and read and think there simply must be more there. We cope with this, of course, by speaking around her, as I will do here. Her poetry has many an accomplished but hardly a provocative line. In fact, Phillis Wheatley holds the distinction of being the most unquotable famous poet in the history of the English language. And there's nothing necessarily wrong with that.

As the variants of her published poems and letters leave clear, she was an exacting and picky writer. Enjambment in her poems is a rare find. She was skilled in bringing together sound and sense. A few textbook examples can be found both in "To Maecenas," in which the line "The length'ning line moves languishing along" is pulled and tugged like an inchworm by the rhythm as the l-words elasticize the meter; and in "On the Death of a Young Lady Five Years of Age," in which the line "Perfect in bliss she from her heav'nly home / looks down" enjambs past the loaded word "home" and down to the first foot of the succeeding line where the spondaic "look down" waits for the reader as she or he looks down to find it. Clever. She was by no means a mockingbird, nor some kind of dumb imitator. She knew precisely what she was doing in a poem and how she wanted to go about doing it. The most prevalent weakness of her poetry was not that she withheld too much of herself, but rather her tendency to weave together two cacophonic tones—the didactic and the obsequious—and yet I can't help but feel that the most injurious thing that happened to her poetry was the mere fact that she was born just before the rise of English Romanticism. Had her models been Coleridge and Byron instead of Pope, had her poems been as loyal to the Romantic ideal as they were to the neoclassical one, we would concern ourselves less with whether Phillis Wheatley was the first, second or fourteenth African-American to publish a book. To dream . . . What happens when you link all of a culture's literary tradition to one writer and one published book, when you pine for an epigraph for the sake of a tradition, is that you acquiesce to italicized ethnography, the poems hold on too well to that role. If only Phillis Wheatley arrived in America a few years later. But alas it didn't happen. And here we are.

Nec gemino bellum Troianum orditur ab ouo semper ad euentum festinat et in medias res. It's undeniable that whatever relevance Phillis Wheatley still has for us today is due to African-American literature's fascination with having an *ab ovo* figure. The mode by which African-American literature thinks itself is deictic and powered by the anthology and the syllabus. Therefore, chronology perhaps unconsciously takes on a disproportionate significance. In this light, we will find that the vast majority of Wheatley criticism centers on the dramatization of the circumstances surrounding the publication of her book. Nothing about it begins in medias res. Phillis Wheatley is handled with an epic tenor but criticism has never been prepared to receive her as a lyric poet.

Phillis Wheatley, like the epigraphs that writers fit into the beginning of their texts, is first and foremost a cultural sign. She is a performance of our imagination, a visual allegory for the various conundrums that African-American literature faces. Next to Langston Hughes, of all African-American poets it is Wheatley's image that is the most familiar and widespread by way of the famed frontispiece of her book. Allegory and allograph, both derived from the same Greek root for the word "other": other speaking and other writing, respectively.

Wheatley's book, despite being a book of poetry, allows for the escape from its content, from poetry itself and into its other the way an epigraph skips forward into the actual text. And this move, the sublimation of verse, or simply the main text's other, into prose—the poetic into the prosaic—now archetypal in African-American literary criticism, is what propels our obsession with firstness and Phillis Wheatley. What we valorize is the context of her work, not its content and in this respect the fact that she wrote poetry, as opposed to say, slave narratives or prose fiction, has not yielded a starting point of its own. We obsess over the existence of Wheatley's book and because of that, paradoxically, we need not worry about the poetry. We have quieted Phillis Wheatley far more than any literary beginning has ever been quieted. We have turned an imagined beginning into an epigraph.

What this tells us, Gérard Genette theorizes, is that "the use of an epigraph is always a mute gesture whose interpretation is left up to the reader."[2] "Phillis Wheatley" as literary figure is by no means mute, but Phillis Wheatley the poet certainly is. On one hand, this should not be much of a concern since poets seem to exist in part to be forgotten and then, perhaps, discovered again, perhaps not; in the end the poets of the future will make their canons. On the other hand, however, Phillis Wheatley is celebrated and has been preserved because she was the first African-American . . . to publish a book. And Jupiter Hammon? And Lucy Terry? Does it not seem somewhat strange that the publication of a book would turn composition entirely into a zero sum game? It is of little surprise the tendency people have to confuse Phillis Wheatley's accomplishment and consider her the first African-American writer ever. It is far more of a surprise to hear a scholar support Wheatley's ubiquity and the absence of her other contemporary poets on qualitative grounds. Phillis Wheatley was not a good enough poet to vanquish anyone into anonymity. To believe otherwise is to indulge in bad faith. What precisely is Phillis Wheatley's value to the African-American literary tradition if not to function as an allegory for the problematic contexts inherent in producing black literature in America? Yet, in order to place her at the head of that tradition and by continually reading her allegorically (especially

2   Gérard Genette, *Paratexts: Thresholds of Interpretation*, trans. Jane E. Lewin (New York: Cambridge University Press, 1997), 156.

considering the voiceless embodiment allegories generally take) she has been practically emptied out of significance as a lyric poet. As Phillis Wheatley is foregrounded as a phenomenon of the plight of black writing, the poet simultaneously wanes into the vehicle of another genre: the prosaic narrative of African-American literature. Phillis Wheatley as an epigraph becomes a trope of our own imagination and subsequent texts. She has become a phenomenon of our own writing.

What does it mean to the African-American literary tradition that Phillis Wheatley was a poet? There was, of course, an inevitability to Wheatley writing poetry in her time. She predated the first American novel, William Hill Brown's *The Power of Sympathy* of 1789. Her inauguration of a new genre weighs heavily against her full commitment to one of the oldest ones. Hence, her poetry pushes backwards away from the tradition she supposedly inaugurates as it pushes forward into it. In this sense Phillis Wheatley pushes forward into chronologies, institutions, and hierarchies while she also pushes back beyond recall.

Perhaps by this point the paucity of Wheatley's poetry within even this discussion will have caught your attention. It is precisely my intention. I wish to demonstrate how Wheatley's work, which is "Phillis Wheatley" (as opposed to the poetry of Phillis Wheatley) functions by means of its mere presence. Aside from being by nature different from the text it precedes, what epigraphs do is fashion a level of significance for either the subsequent text or the author, sometimes both. But the main function of an epigraph is not to signify (what writer wants to be outdone by a few lines by another writer?). Instead the central function of an epigraph is to simply be there. Its mere being is charged with significance and gives a glimpse into the intended affect of the writer. It need not do more than this. Gérard Genette coined the phrase "a password of intellectuality" in describing the epigraph as that through which the author "chooses his peers and thus his place in the pantheon." The epigraph is a "paratext," according to Genette: a threshold (as opposed to a boundary) of transition and transaction in which the value properties of the main text are enhanced by the paratext. Consider, for example, my editor using the first line of *A Tale of Two Cities* as an epigraph to my novel about growing up playing basketball. The brief gesture at the beginning of the novel then would suggest bittersweet reflection, intense conflict perhaps allegorized to the extent of war, and perhaps class conflict. But it also would strongly imply my familiarity with one of the great novels of the language, it would either color my novel as an attempt at "serious" literature or out me as being naive (or possibly coy) enough to begin a novel with what's likely the most famous first line of any novel ever written. Regardless, it would first and foremost do something simply in being there. Its presence would fashion the text and the author, locating both with an acute context. Consider the difference: same novel about basketball, a line from a rap song. "The most powerful oblique effect of the epigraph is perhaps due simply to its presence, whatever the epigraph itself may be: this is the epigraph-effect. The presence or absence of an epigraph in itself marks (with a very thin margin of error) the period, the genre, or the tenor of a piece of writing."[3]

Genette's work mirrors the curious case by which Phillis Wheatley slips from subject to object. She is simultaneously the

---

3   Genette, *Paratexts*, 160.

focus of the emergence of the writing subject, and the objectified allegory of that event of writing. Thus, most writing on Phillis Wheatley is engaged with the non-written elements of her work: she is the axle usually of a discussion without being the axis or the wheel, she is a structure whose context moves but does not experience motion. "The epigraph is most often allographic, that is according to our conventions, attributed to an author who is not the author of the work."[4] In such instances, African-American poetics reveals the extent to which it is under duress, for its archetypes (the allegories of Wheatley, Hughes, and the bluesman) are stuck under other ways of speaking, which has a textual equivalent of being stuck between title and text.

Is Phillis Wheatley's poetry a part of this beginning, or is it—this beginning—the very fact of her writing, the controlled public performance of her authorship, and its subsequent reliance upon the modernity of the book? Similar to the epigraph, Phillis Wheatley is an enabling vehicle. Thus, pronouncements of Phillis Wheatley's "place" in an African-American literary tradition also require that we recognize the poet as a foregone conclusion: an effect which marks as much the constructed presence of the poet and what that poet signifies as of the text itself. We engage Phillis Wheatley, in other words, in an act of authentication ironically similar to that of the authenticating documents which appendage Wheatley's *Poems on Various Subjects, Religious and Moral* of 1773.

Phillis Wheatley is a phenomenon. Phillis Wheatley is an event. She is recalled more for the contexts of her poetry than for her

---

4   Genette, *Paratexts*, 151.

poetry. Who has put Phillis Wheatley's poems to heart, or thinks to use any of her lines to describe a situation that is not Phillis Wheatley's situation? What poet can we say has been influenced by Phillis Wheatley save for those poets such as Jupiter Hammon, Robert Hayden, June Jordan, and Naomi Long Madgett who have written poems directly *about* Phillis Wheatley. And if the easily digestible answer is that we have all been influenced by Phillis Wheatley, then what you are really saying is that we have all been influenced by the phenomenological value of the book. Why are we then not influenced by Lucy Terry or Jupiter Hammon or George Moses Horton? Indeed, Phillis Wheatley is a sign of context much more so than content or form. Strangely, she is at the center of African-American literary discourse and adamantly outside of it. At this point it is quite clear that Phillis Wheatley exists in a synecdochal relationship to an African-American literary tradition: her parts (that which is *poetic*) represent the straining toward a whole (that which is *prosaic*, or the manner in which this tradition envisions itself subversively in terms of narrative prose).

In many respects, as this chapter's epigraph attempts to allude to, Phillis Wheatley is a thin shadow in the memory (a counterintuitive claim given her growing popularity among literary historians). As epigraphs seek to further illuminate the texts they antecede, even the thinnest of shadows affirms an object's presence in the light. That it is through prose and history, instead of through poems, that we most often engage Phillis Wheatley says as much about where African-American poetry is today in the grand scheme of literary criticism as has any literary scholarship thus far written on the subject of African-American poetry itself.

While absence has been codified into a readable source of intellectual and artistic activity, it is the absence of a developing field of poetics where poetry itself must be at the crux of the subject that is the absence still rendered as intangible. I am not looking here to sound an elegy for poetry, or an indictment of an underappreciated group of minority poets (though both options, admittedly, would be enticing). Instead, I presume a single, and rather simple question: If Phillis Wheatley was a poet and is a celebrated figure, why then is there so little to say about Phillis Wheatley's poetry? What does it mean that we still speak so comfortably of Phillis Wheatley without having to engage her poetry at all?

Woman. Black. Poet. Slave. House Slave. How many identities does Phillis Wheatley's presence fill? If, like an epigraph, Wheatley projects the gap between the title ("the African-American literary tradition") and its text (the published books that have followed), then her presence likewise offers a constructed pleasure. In terms outlined by Roland Barthes in his *The Pleasure of the Text*, pleasure (*plaisir*) serves as moderate enjoyment and passive consumption of texts in a manner that reenacts suitable cultural codes. *Jouissance* meanwhile calls up a possible malestrom of stimuli: loss, death, climactic bliss, maenadic violence. Pleasure offers the possibility of tradition as a steady chronology of texts, and suggests that teleological surge underlying what "the African-American literary tradition" seeks to signify. *Jouissance* is, at its most basic, the risk of a descent toward an incurable philistinism.

The point of Wheatley's presence as the inaugural author within this literary tradition serves to indicate the ability of a published text to transcend slavery. This is the action of reassurance; it is the work of pleasure. As opposed to the more Dionysian *jouissance*, this pleasure—that in the end may be subjective, aesthetic, or just flatly ideological—self-fashions a mode of reading Phillis Wheatley as a starting point, as a suitable beginning, as a calming text from whence to start. The idea of Wheatley's book coupled with Wheatley's image yield the safe illusion that one is participating in an origin, in some terribly flawed beginning in which—as though one saw the head of Orpheus floating down the river and chased it to re-attach it to the flayed body—one can somehow, someway, make the very idea of blacks writing in English in the New World a whole, manageable, narrative of author, and identity. Wheatley's book and image give us the illusion that we participate in some flawed beginning, which we, by acknowledging it as tradition, supposedly confront and resolve.

So we know of Phillis Wheatley as an enterprise of firsts. From this age of self-conscious succession, where we mark the "post" before so many ways of representing the world, the fact that we are now "post-Phillis Wheatley" yet in terms of criticism nearly consumed by her, contextualizes the extent to which we treat this poet as a set of extremes.

Henry Louis Gates, Jr.:
The birth of the Afro-American literary tradition occurred in 1773, when Phillis Wheatley published a book of poetry. *Despite the fact that . . .* [5]

---

5   Henry Louis Gates, Jr., "Foreword: In Her Own Write," in Phillis Wheatley, *The Collected Poems of Phillis Wheatley*, ed. John C. Shields (New York: Oxford University Press, 1987), vii. Italics added.

June Jordan:
It was *not* natural. And she was the first.[6]

Julian D. Mason, Jr.:
Phillis Wheatley was *not* the first black American to publish. For example, Briton Hammon preceded her with a fourteen-page pamphlet in 1760 (his only publication); and Jupiter Hammon published an eighty-eight-line poem praising Wheatley after she was already well established as a poet. Certainly she was the first truly significant black American writer, and her 1773 book of poems was probably the first book—and certainly the first book of poetry—published by a black American.[7]

Nellie Y. McKay:
The American edition of *Poems on Various Subjects, Religious and Moral* was published in Philadelphia in 1786, *four years after her death.*[8]

These come from two introductions for different editions of Wheatley's collected poetry, one creative essay, and one article from *PMLA* on the state of African-American affairs in the academy. Note that all of them concern themselves with firstness and the epigraphic mood. But we must note as well how firstness is

---

FOOTNOTE

6   June Jordan, "The Difficult Miracle of Black Poetry in America or Something like a Sonnet for Phillis Wheatley," *Massachusetts Review* 27:2 (1986): 252.
7   Julian D. Mason, Jr., "Introduction," in Phillis Wheatley, *The Poems of Phillis Wheatley*, ed. Julian D. Mason, Jr. (Chapel Hill: The University of North Carolina Press, 1989), 13. Italics added.
8   Nellie Y. McKay, "Naming the Problem that Led to the Question 'Who Shall Teach African American Literature?'; or Are We Ready to Disband the Wheatley Court?," *PMLA* 113:3 (1998): 360. Italics added.

propelled by negation, the mood of which is what dramatizes how the very notion of a beginning for African-American literature is fraught with a tragic significance and is bound by a hovering threat of its own failure. Firstness, the analeptic conceit, makes the stakes of Wheatley's solvency not a matter of the poet's verses but of the solvency of the canon itself. Hence the stakes of the poet's life are caught in the issues of threat to canon-foundation that, for a canon so sparsely attentive to its poetry, quickly becomes an issue revolving around prose.

This threat in origin is echoed in what Slavoj Žižek refers to as "dealing with a *failed* logic, with an endlessly repeated effort to begin."[9] It is precisely this "endless oscillation between contraction and expansion" that leaves Wheatley "propelled by the impossibility of formulating the 'stable' relationship between S[ubject] and P[redicate] that forms the structure of a propositional judgment: the subject (also and above all in the logical sense of the term) 'contracts' itself and annihilates its predicative content, whereas in the ensuing gesture of expansion it passes over into the predicate and thereby loses the firmer ground of its self-consistency."[10]

Imagine the predicative content in this case to be poetic criticism on Wheatley. Losing "the firmer ground of its self-consistency," a sustained poetic understanding of Wheatley's relevance deliquesces and loses any possibility of a "stable" relationship at the point of convergence between "S and P" particularly in the vein of S signifying S[cholarship] and P P[oetry]. S[cholarship] thus "contracts" itself around the dominant ideology of prosaic

---

9   Slavoj Žižek and F.W.J. von Schelling, *The Abyss of Freedom / Ages of the World*, trans. Judith Norman (Ann Arbor: The University of Michigan Press, 1997), 19.
10   Žižek and von Schelling, *Abyss of Freedom*, 19–20.

reading, treating all texts as narrative prose and annihilating any possible significant poetic content while feigning through deictic utterance the gesture of "expansion" toward P[oetry].

Phillis Wheatley in this regard is a paradigmatic trope of criticism's obsession with simultaneously the creation of an origin and the refutation of that same origin. Phillis Wheatley is a slave who published a book of poems—from that point on African-American literary tradition consists largely of: individuals who were enslaved, took their freedom and wrote a narrative on it; then individuals who were free yet sensed their confinement and wrote a narrative to explain their sense of it; then individuals who were free yet sensed their confinement and wrote a narrative to confound the reader's sense of it. Everything leads to a manner of *not being Phillis Wheatley.*

When Gates rightly arrives at the question, "What would happen if we ceased to stereotype Wheatley but, instead, read her, read her with all the resourcefulness that she herself brought to her craft?" his sense of the problem as being one of stereotyping is telling. The time for boomeranging buzzwords for this particular problem, which is an artistic problem, has passed. Simply put, the problem with our study of Wheatley is not one of stereotypes, it is a problem of genre. And if genre, particularly the genre of poetry, had been paid more critical attention to in the first place, then a mere plea for close reading would have hardly been necessary.

The outcome of this desire to begin with Phillis Wheatley is a series of prosaic encounters with a number of allegorical interpretive contexts: the very material of the book of a slave, the narrative of her highly particularized literary history, the antagonistic relationship between the authoritative command of the book's attestations and the authorial presence of the poet, and the transcendent allegorizing (either privileged or disparaged) of this author's plight in our own era of writing. One of the more fertile and certainly more muted sites of this type of conflict occurs at the discursive ledge where poetry and prose meet. This conflict between one form of blackness (verse as origin) and another form of blackness (prose as an end) configures the vital crux, often unheard and unheeded, through which African-American literature has formed its identity. It is at this epistrophic ledge where the drama of blackness attempting its conflicted rhyme with blackness occurs. The risk is being swallowed whole by sameness and repetition. The reward is encountering the enabling hominy of blackness rhyming with blackness.

African-American literary study has premised writing to be the antithesis of the objectified, de-humanized "without" rendered upon the slave. However, to think of "writing" without a sense of genre is to focus on act and not on art; this is no tradition, only activity. "Writing" must be supplemented by genre, and hopefully complimented as well by mode. When it is not, the very idea that writing is a form of freedom is laid to waste: if writing is to be taken seriously as a vital part of the writing subject's move towards a self-realized autonomy, then *what* was written—the notion of generic choice—must play its crucial role. This means not only *what* in terms of close reading, but also *what* and *how*. Is not self-determined individuality about the power to choose? African-American literary study must focus more on genre in part because genre not only reflects the values placed in a given literary environment, it also reflects upon choice.

Thus, that Phillis Wheatley wrote poems during an emergent age of prose needs to be considered alongside the fact that, as a lyric poet, Wheatley was engaged in a conflict of two types of discourse which are not primarily slave and writing (slaves had been writing for thousands of years, including African slaves) but slave and verse. The case of Phillis Wheatley was not about slave versus "writing," it was about slave versus verse.

Phillis Wheatley in this sense is the unavoidable trope of the problematic beginning of the book as it has pertained to the forming of an African-American literary canon that functions antithetically to the lyric. Whether we like it or not, 18th century poetry is where African-American literature begins. We will eventually have to turn more toward the lyric and shake off this epigraphic mood. When Genette writes of the taste for the epigraph as being a symptom of the growing infatuation with the novel, he is close in sentiment (and era) to making a direct statement on Phillis Wheatley as a meta-epigraph.

> People have rightly seen the epigraphic excess of the early nineteenth century as a desire to integrate the novel, particularly the historical or "philosophical" novel, into a cultural tradition. The young writers of the 1960s and 1970s used the same means to give themselves the consecration and unction of a(nother) prestigious filiation.[11]

Phillis Wheatley authorizes a way of speaking that is antithetical and, dare I say, carnivorous to the slight body of her own work.

---

11 Genette, *Paratexts*, 160.

Consequently, poetry loses its sense of signification within African-American literature's emergent sense of "writing" and "history"—both of which configure the possible rendering of all successive poetic signs as meaningless. Poetry exists within African-American literature not on the margins but rather as epigraphic material, which may be a worse fate. Again, arguing for the marginalization of African-American poetry would only lead us back into the same debates of inclusion and exclusion. Instead, greater focus should be paid to the epigraphic mood of poetry in African-American literary discourse. A discourse that understands prose as its metonymic sign for literature. Poetry under this paradigm is introductory, referential, and—as all epigraphs are—non-committal. As can be seen by the manner in which Wheatley functions as a contextual instead of a formal referent to the tradition she inaugurates, poetry in terms of the African-American literary tradition serves first and foremost as a paratextual embellishment for the benefits of prose. By referring to the epigraph as allographic writing, Genette alludes to the calligraphic (or high-embellishment) of the extra writing bounding textual borders. James Elkins, in his book on visual communication and semiotics, *The Domain of Images*, views allographs in terms of modern Western culture's tendency toward a visual ornamentation of text (or, in this case of writing, letters).

It is as if the letters were a firm foundation, fixed in shape and denotation, and the allographs merely embellishment. That at least is the way calligraphy has traditionally been understood in the post-Renaissance West: it is an optional refinement, and takes whatever meaning it has from the history of the ornament and from the insecure symbolism of gestures and patterns.[12]

It is difficult to resist the impression that the prioritized genre through which we regard Wheatley is pre-textual and hardly poetic. As Christopher Felker writes, "in the making of Wheatley's poetry, there can be no meaning without noticing its pretext."[13] I by no means seek to compromise the criticism that has throughout the years focused upon Wheatley's poetry first and foremost, yet I do maintain that these studies are for the most part extra-textual and outside the bounds of Wheatley criticism's relevance to African-American literary criticism as it discloses itself. The allograph that encapsulates Wheatley is read allegorically as "the history of the ornament" and is shaped by a hermeneutic of the non-poetic aspects of Wheatley's book: the Attestation, the image of the author, and the material facticity (the historicized version of that same moment Sartre would call "thingness") of the book itself. With these three components, and these three alone, one is provided with the vast bulk, the very centripetal force of Wheatley's figuration. Accordingly, when Daniel Cottom argues that Wheatley's frontispiece is in actuality the authorizing document of Wheatley's status, he states that

> [i]n fact, although the design of the book has the Attestation coming after the portrait, this document logically

---

12   James Elkins, *The Domain of Images* (Ithaca: Cornell University Press, 1999), 95.
13   Christopher Felker, "'The Tongues of the learned are insufficient': Phillis Wheatley, Publishing Objectives, and Personal Liberty," in *Texts and Textuality: Textual Instability, Theory, and Interpretation*, ed. Philip Cohen (New York: Routledge, 1997), 85.

must be considered to precede Wheatley's image, since we can infer that the book would not have been published or even attributed to "Phillis Wheatley" if the judgement of these men had gone against her. The portrait has its place at the beginning of the volume, then, but then again, it is there only in lieu of the real placeholders, who determine its proper position to be after and under their own names.[14]

Yet this inclination to contest one form of non-literary representation within the book (the Attestation) with another (the frontispiece) falsely sets at odds two aspects of *Poems on Various Subjects, Religious and Moral* that are at work together. Both figures defer the poetic matter of the text, once deferred by audience and again deferred by a distracting and contrived blackness captioned by the frontispiece.

The high level of iconicity—her frontispiece, her inalienable blackness—embedded within the significance of Wheatley's volume inevitably conspired against the verse it contained. Northrop Frye has argued that lyric poetry and imagery were common and useful companions: "there are thousands of lyrics so intently focused on visual imagery that they are, as we may say, set to pictures." Frye went on to argue that as with "the emblem an actual picture appears," providing the poem with a vital associative quality.[15] The overdetermination of Wheatley's very image by her audience would have an undeniable effect on the figural function

14 Daniel Cottom, *Ravishing Tradition: Cultural Forces and Literary History* (Ithaca: Cornell University Press, 1996), 92.
15 Northrop Frye, *Anatomy of Criticism: Four Essays* (Princeton: Princeton University Press, 1957), 274.

of her lyric poetry. It is a simple equation, if Frye is to assume that pictorialism supplements the structural interpretation of the lyric, then distinct figural history of black images in the minds of readers would then likewise re-order the significance of the lyric. This pictorial resonance, while centered on Wheatley's blackness as a captioned epigraph to her volume of verse, concerns more than just a visual text. The attestation still proves to be another context by which one reads prose as a paraphrase for poetry's significance, or perhaps I should say, of each poem's significance. For the metonymic reduction of each poem's worth, syllable by syllable, allusion by allusion, is sanctioned first and foremost, if not singularly, by these two non-poetic texts: one visual and the other prose-catalogue.

Consequently, readers of Wheatley from both the past and present engage in an act of misreading; not by way of interpretation, but rather by genre. When recuperated by contemporary scholarship, what promotes a supposedly fresh idea of Wheatley is rarely a matter of the genre specific to the subject (and what, then, is the point of keeping alive the subject?). What makes for the possibility critics cherish—Wheatley's epigraphic and inaugural significance—is that the subject streamlines into current academic debates, most of which run counter to, or ignore completely, poetic arguments. "Wheatley's poems," Kristin Wilcox writes, "are now chained to issues of canonicity and literary merit; the supposedly authentic literary voice recuperated by close reading is opposed to the often clumsy and derivative neoclassicism of her less successful verses."[16] Are Wheatley's

16 Kristin Wilcox, "The Body into Print: Marketing Phillis Wheatley," *American Literature* 71:1 (1991): 2.

poems really "chained" by the dialectic of counter-subversive prose paraphrases and the mere close readings of her "clumsy and derivative" poems? Yes and no. Phillis Wheatley works best as "Phillis Wheatley," a closed set of non-poetic signifiers that allegorize as a poetics of beginning. "Poetics" in this instance functions as a phenomenon that counterintuitively renders Phillis Wheatley's poetry in the middle of an annihilating crux: that her poetry is, as Wilcox has aptly put it "simultaneously possible and irrelevant."

What was and has endured throughout the years in appraising the work of Phillis Wheatley has not been the quality of her verse, this is quite clear. African-American literary studies has developed non-poetic criteria by which to sustain its inaugural poet: the allegorical image of blackness captioned, wistful, elusive (what is it, after all, that Wheatley is writing in this picture and why is her book closed?), mediated through the writing of the Attestation. However, the Attestation also functioned contemporaneously as an allegorical text for its white readers in London and then Boston. If the Attestation affirmed the authenticity of Wheatley's poems it also circumscribes, if not captions, their aesthetic merit. The Attestation transmogrifies what it supposedly authenticates, not simply along racist lines of power but within generic ones as well. Hence, like other ancillary writings surrounding Wheatley's verses, such as copies of the advertisement laid out for the volume by Wheatley's London publisher Archibald Bell, all ancillary texts that accompany *Poems on Various Subjects, Religious and Moral*—all of them—are concerned largely with the translation and corroboration of power.

The late eighteenth century was a ripe moment for this type of mis-reading as the era leaned increasingly toward the novel. It was more prepared than ever before to supplement and then replace the aesthetic problem of Wheatley (that she was a lyric poet) with the aesthetic narrative of Wheatley, which persisted in having its ultimate referent on the margin of the book. Counter to what one may infer from this assertion, I do not believe that intensive close reading would solve the problem herein outlined. Instead, I am claiming that while Wheatley criticism has provided numerous ways to consider the ideological underpinnings of texts previously thought of as hermeneutically sealed, there is still the fact that though non-poetic texts such as the Attestation and the frontispiece have been incorporated into critical discourses to confound previously held notions of race, gender, and history, they still function in the same manner generically. These texts still perform much of the same work that they did in their original contexts of the late eighteenth century. This is because the particularities of poetry are not read as a difference, but rather are read indifferently.

There are numerous reasons why the era between the decline of Pope and the rise of English Romanticism is regarded as the age of prose. It was a period of major transatlantic transitions as the publishing and purchasing interests in both Britain and America evinced a greater (and perhaps more populist) interest in the novel and its necessary arbiter, the book. In England, with the death of Queen Anne, courtly patronage of poetry was practically at an end (which is something we should always keep in mind when considering the dynamics of Nathaniel and

Phillis Wheatley's 1773 visit to London in order to secure the patronage of the Countess of Huntingdon) and accordingly, poets were by the 1770s more at the mercy of a transitional book market consisting of capitalist booksellers and a new middle-class reading audience. "The rising middle class," writes Cathy N. Davidson, "with its increasingly voracious appetite for books, especially novels, portended a new mass patronage of books based not on a work's appeal to the gentry but on its general popularity."[17]

Readers at this time were not at the mere whim of authors, rather authors became objects of the fancy of a reading public governed now more than ever by the imagination of the market, as opposed to the imagination of the singular and isolated mind. Though Wheatley's book circulated among, and was authenticated by, the landed classes of London and Boston, it entered a capitalist market in which the whimsy of the gentry was inevitably to mingle with the whimsy of the other classes. Davidson notes that "there is evidence that those of modest to low income increasingly read many books" and that this was due in no small part to the institutionalization of free libraries and a growing common habit of book borrowing, which was "singularly intertwined with not just the rapid growth of reading and readerships but with an increasing demand for novels."[18] Therefore—although Susanna Wheatley encouraged Wheatley's love of Pope, Ovid, and most certainly Horace, and though Wheatley clearly sought to establish for herself a

---

17   Cathy N. Davidson, *Revolution and the Word: The Rise of the Novel in America* (New York: Oxford, 1986), 16.
18   Ibid., 27.

reputation as a "poet" as opposed to a "writer"—the work of the book within larger contexts was a counterfoil to this poetic ambition. *Poems on Various Subjects, Religious and Moral*, as opposed to the courtier poems that preceded Wheatley and the nudgingly courtly poems she penned for individual publication, spun within an evolving matrix of cultural forces prepared for the consumption of the text within its emergent habit of prosaic reading.

As though aware of this paradox, the circulation of Wheatley's book was intended to be a particular endeavor designed to reinforce the more traditional sense of her work as belonging to an older way of literature being more effuse than object. To this end, however, it was decided that the visual image of Wheatley was indispensable to giving the sense of the work as high art, thus placing the non-poetic material into even greater focus. As Christopher Felker has found,

> Wheatley's book was marketed principally as a literature for "extensive" reading and sold principally in urban port cities (most notably Boston) that dominated long-distance communications. The precise cultural character of communications and commerce in Northern Ports is important for understanding the reception of Wheatley's work. The Wheatleys were among that group described by David Hall as "beginning to withdraw from [the] common world into a new gentility. The coming of gentlemen's libraries, together with dancing assemblies, the tea ceremony, and the theatre, were steps in the making of a cosmopolitan alternative to the culture of tra-

ditional literacy" ("The Uses of Literacy in New England" 45). Wheatley's *Poems on Various Subjects* was originally intended to circulate in this world, and so it was important to the Countess of Huntingdon that the book contain a fine engraving. The engraving was only the most obvious example of a textual feature designed to convince purchasers that Wheatley's poems were more than a "book"; these poems were "literature." *Poems on Various Subjects* was intended for a fashion-minded clientele prepared to buy the book on "impulse."[19]

Thus, I would like to offer two points. The first being that the difficulty endured by Wheatley in originally gaining an ear for her proposals (she offered four: one each in 1772, 1773, 1779 and 1783) was in some measure a matter of poetry suffering, on both sides of the Atlantic, a wane of interest. Quite a fair number of readers likely managed an initial interest in the work of Wheatley only to turn away in disappointment upon the discovery that, as Marquis de Barbé-Marbois described her, "one of the strangest creatures . . . perhaps in the whole world" wrote calm, temperate verse; which in the end may not have meant the end of "Phillis Wheatley" for them but would have made her a discourse of "matter" or existence, rather than of poems or poetry. We should regard the Marquis, stationed in America from 1779–1785, as an outside reader to this phenomenon. He was more an ideal reader than most, not only giving praise to the poems but also actually telling of his experience in reading them; though even in his letter, which I shall

---

19   Felker, " 'The Tongues of the learned are insufficient,' " 81–120.

quote at length, one should note how the experience of reading Wheatley's poetry is circumscribed in the beginning and end by, respectively, a paraphrase of her biography and a tactile experience with the book as the real, the verifying and verified, object encountered.

> Phyllis [*sic*] is a negress, born in Africa, brought to Boston at the age of ten, and sold to a citizen of that city. She learned English with unusual ease, eagerly read and reread the Bible, the only book which had been put in her hands, became steeped in the poetic images of which it is full, and at the age of seventeen published a number of poems in which there is imagination, poetry, and zeal, though no correctness nor order of interest. I read them with some surprise. They are printed and in the front of the book there are certificates of authenticity which leave no doubt that she is its author . . .[20]

Though what is attested to is thus supposedly confirmed as real, Wheatley's poems lack any of the pyrotechnics of the seduction novel, the captive narrative, or the travel narrative. As the novel develops the desire of its readers, Patricia Meyer Spacks has argued, "truth" comes at the expense of reality. Plot, in other words, "calls attention to the importance of truth—not realism: *truth*—as an issue in fiction."[21] And for that very reason Phillis Wheatley's story is less real, for as its veracity is attested

---

20   Marquis de Barbé-Marbois, letter, 28 August 1779, in *Critical Essays on Phillis Wheatley*, ed. William H. Robinson (Boston: G. K. Hall and Co., 1982), 37.
21   Patricia Meyer Spacks, *Desire and Truth: Functions of Plot in Eighteenth-Century Novels* (Chicago: The University of Chicago Press, 1990), 1–2.

to by an outside authorial presence, the imagination of the common eighteenth-century reader is set up to resist the possibility of writing and worse yet, must suffer this resistance within a genre increasingly less fashionable. For every favorable review of Wheatley, there was an unfavorable one. For every elegy (elegies comprise over a third of her volume) there is a reminder of the elegy's overwrought, over-poeticized treatment of death. We find this in mock-elegies by poets as prominent as Gray and Goldsmith in their "Ode on the Death of a Favorite Cat, Drowned in a Tub of Goldfishes" and "Elegy on the Death of a Mad Dog" of 1748 and 1766 respectively. The new fictions of the eighteenth century were by and large texts of desire and accordingly provided something closer to a teleological sense of the truth: goals in the form of social codes were attained or tragically lost. Wheatley's *Poems on Various Subjects* in this world worked as it does now, particularly because in both situations it is read for plot. Spacks, discussing the general desire for ends in eighteenth-century novels, strikes a chord also at the heart of the phenomenon of Phillis Wheatley. "Among the most potent human desires, one must number the desire for teleology, afflicting readers and writers alike. Fictional plots appear to move toward appointed ends, and so do the narratives of literary history."[22]

Wheatley's predecessor of sorts is Oroonoko. But who can forget Oroonoko's prefacing promise to "not pretend, in giving you the history of this royal slave, to entertain my reader with adventures of a feign'd hero, whose life and fortunes fancy may manage at the poet's pleasure; nor in relating the truth,

22   Spacks, *Desire and Truth*, 237–8.

design to adorn it with any accidents, but such as arrived in earnest to him." On the cusp of a literary sea change of readership and genre, it was fiction and the novel—not fancy and the couplet—that fashioned the readership of Wheatley's time. With novels such as Daniel Defoe's *Robinson Crusoe* (1719) and *Moll Flanders* (1722), Eliza Haywood's *The Fatal Secret, or Constancy in Distress* (1724), Henry Fielding's *Tom Jones* (1749), and Samuel Richardson's *Clarissa* (1747–8), by the time of Wheatley's appearance the eighteenth century was well on its path to distinguish itself as an era during which prose, and specifically the novel, would replace poetry's reign over moral debate and good old-fashioned fun. "Reason, moderation, good sense, and the scientific outlook were the ideals of the eighteenth century," James Reeves wrote, "they require the existence of a perspicuous and flexible prose, but they are apt to produce dull poetry."[23]

So, surrounded by prose on all sides, where in the world does Phillis Wheatley fit? She is so easily summed up, the gist of her so quickly digested, you almost end up having the sensation that Phillis Wheatley is herself all fiction. And in a sense, she has become so. Read as the plot of an entire literature she is the paraphrase of the problems of our literary lives today, as she was of the institutional ills of the new republic. As with this essay itself, she is full of signification—she signifies the start of an entire literary tradition—yet she is so most through a sublime silence on her part. As with the epigraph, she is part of the text but not, you feel, part of the equation.

---

23   James Reeves, *A Short History of English Poetry: 1340–1940* (New York: E. P. Dutton and Co., 1964), 123.

Swallowed whole by self-satisfying interpretations of rhetorical resistance or historical construction, where Wheatley becomes in either case an intimate insider, Wheatley's presence melds the tendency of these trends: prosaic. In this sense we are critically where we left off with Phillis Wheatley, she is a beginning and an end, sent to cure our ills, whatever they may be. She is Prose's peculiar child, a mysterious Athena, a cephalic birth from our literature's hard, ever-altering, prosaic head.

"MY FIRST GLIMMERING CONCEPTION":
FREDERICK DOUGLASS AND THE LIMITS OF PROSE

When it is finally ours, this freedom, this liberty, this beautiful
and terrible thing, needful to man as air,
useable as earth; when it belongs at last to all,
when it is truly instinct, brain matter, diastole, systole,
reflex action; when it is finally won; when it is more
than the gaudy mumbo jumbo of politicians:
this man, this Douglass, this former slave, this Negro
beaten to his knees, exiled, visioning a world
where none is lonely, none hunted, alien,
this man, superb in love and logic, this man
shall be remembered. Oh, not with statues' rhetoric,
not with legends and poems and wreaths of bronze alone,
but with the lives grown out of his life, the lives
fleshing his dream of the beautiful needful thing.[24]

---

24   Robert Hayden, "Frederick Douglass," *The Collected Poems of Robert Hayden*
(New York: Liveright, 1985), 62.

43

I

When, finally, it was his—that freedom, that liberty, that thing needful as air, useable as earth—Frederick Douglass looked back on his life and wrote of his years of enslavement. *Narrative of the Life of Frederick Douglass, An American Slave Written by Himself* was published by the Anti-Slavery office in Boston in 1845, four years after Douglass had become a salaried lecturer for the Massachusetts Anti-Slavery Society and some seven years after he had escaped from bondage with borrowed papers from American merchant seamen. The reasons that led Douglass to publish his life story have been well documented. In brief: Douglass had developed a well-earned reputation as a tremendous public orator on behalf of the abolitionist movement; but, to his displeasure, his speeches were often vetted in advance by his colleagues. Add to this a chorus of skeptics who doubted the veracity of his amazing and heartbreaking stories. Douglass came to feel in time that he was being held back by the limits of public oration. He would require a far larger platform.

The *Narrative* would end up being a tremendous—and sustained—success, selling five thousand copies within the first four months of publication and close to sixty thousand copies over the next fifteen years (which takes us to the year preceding the Civil War). It has long been considered the locus classicus of the slave narrative, and rightfully so. And what of the fact that Douglass both became a writer and published his book during one of the pivotal eras of American poetry? The *Narrative* surfaced within a year of Emerson's "The Poet" and Poe's *The Raven and Other Poems*. Ten years later, in 1855, Douglass's second autobiography,

My Bondage, My Freedom, would be published along with two books of poetry that sold terribly: Whitman's *Leaves of Grass* and, across the Atlantic, Browning's *Men and Women.*

Like Phillis Wheatley, Frederick Douglass was surrounded by poetry. But while Wheatley was contending with a set of fixed poetic styles and a general readership increasingly enthralled by the novel, Douglass settled comfortably into being a non-fiction writer at a time when American poetry was slowly freeing its rhythms. But how, if at all, did the poetic climate affect the man who would come to be known as the most famous black in the world? We will be discussing here how Douglass was a writer troubled to his core by an antagonistic interplay between the poetry and prose, the poetic and the prosaic, in his work. A close look into Douglass's first autobiography will reveal the lengths to which Douglass's prose was affected by poetic representation and mis-representation.

II

Slave verse—the singing of slaves, an oral poetry with no blueprint for how it should look on the page, how its melisma may fit a meter, how incremental repetition or call and response should be arranged into stanzas—posed an unavoidable formal problem to narrative of that time: how to put it down in print. There were two pragmatic options:[25] it could be transcribed into stanzas and rendered like any lyric poem; or, it could be paraphrased to fit

---

25 A third more idiosyncratic option would be to interpret the singing onto a diatonic scale and then transcribe it as musical notation, which ended up happening. This will be discussed later.

into prose. Douglass chose option two. We are early in Douglass's life as a writer: the second chapter of his first biography. This archetypal moment in the creation of Douglass's authorial (and authoritative) voice is already renown for its unique poignancy and power in describing the existential life of slaves on a plantation. However, we will be discussing Chapter Two of the *Narrative* for different reasons and on different terms. For it is one of the most unique and vital defenses of American poetry that has ever been written. It is a defense of a new lyrical form's existence before it even existed as a lyrical form.

Douglass ended up writing two more autobiographies after the *Narrative* of 1845: *My Bondage and My Freedom* appeared in 1855 and *The Life and Times of Frederick Douglass* was published in 1881. Douglass, born in 1818, was coming of age not only during one of the more pivotal moments in the history of American poetry, as was stated above, but also during one of the most divided moments in American poetry. On one side there was Emerson and on the other side was Poe. Emerson in his essays and poems championed the transcendent power of poetry to steer the mind toward truth and self-realization. For Poe, who Emerson thought of as a "jingling serenader," each poem desired to exist on a sensuous level of its own making. Poetry, according to Poe, does not strive to be natural or to be a part of us; instead it revels in its separateness: it is a crafted object, often set to syllables, and always manifesting *"an elevating excitement of the Soul*—quite independent of that passion which is the intoxication of the Heart—or of that Truth which is the satisfaction of Reason."[26]

---

26   Edgar Allan Poe, "The Poetic Principle," *The Fall of the House of Usher and Other Writings* (New York: Penguin, 1986), 511.

The lines drawn in the American soil by Emerson (devout Northerner) and Poe (conflicted and transplanted Southerner) regarding Truth, Reason, and their place within an American poetry is perhaps the most apt metaphor for American poetry's teetering attempt to gather itself as the nation itself teetered on the edge of disunion. Yet more and more the tenets argued over by Emerson and Poe began to play themselves out not in poetry, but in prose. If the eighteenth century provided the groundwork for an American love of prose and plot, then the nineteenth century supplied the edifice. While "Transcendental Poets," "Fireside Poets," and "Household Poets" continued to publish and be placed on the bookshelves of faux-Victorian homes, there was an increasing sense among the American public that "poetry tended, in spite of Wordsworth's prefaces, to become divorced from 'knowledge,' which, with the drift of the nineteenth century, become more and more the special province of science."[27]

The nineteenth century American poet was to an extent in conflict with a new America where, as Eric Haralson writes, "the poet must confront 'active' 'real' life, so that he could then rally other men—whether merchants, playwrights, or attorneys—to do likewise, and to *keep* doing likewise. His poetry must aim, as Bryant said, at 'the incitement to vigorous toils endured for the welfare of communities.'"[28] Meanwhile, the incredible popularity of a new genre, the slave narrative, was satisfying a niche in the reading public. "The great antebellum works of Ralph Waldo Emerson, Henry David Thoreau, Walt Whitman, Herman Melville,

---

27   F. O. Matthiessen, *The American Renaissance: Art and Expression in the Age of Emerson and Whitman* (New York: Oxford, 1972), 247.
28   Eric L. Haralson, "Mars in Petticoats: Longfellow and Sentimental Masculinity," *Nineteenth Century American Literature* 51:3 (1996): 334.

or Margaret Fuller did not sell nearly as well as the approximately one hundred book-length slave narratives," David W. Blight confirms.[29] In fact, between 1840 and 1860, William Wells Brown (1842), Lunford Lane (1842), Moses Grandy (1844), Frederick Douglass (1845), Lewis Clarke (1846), Henry Bibb (1849), J. W. C. Pennington (1850), Solomon Northup (1853), Austin Steward, and J. W. Loguen (1859) all published narratives recounting their lives under the oppression of slavery.

Despite being first and foremost an encounter with pervasive difference—an individual thought to be less than human recounting that life to you on deeply human terms—acceptance of the slave narratives to the literary culture of the nineteenth century does not emphasize a difference of writing. On the contrary, the public acceptance of "the narrative" places it in a similar-yet-different relation to the novel. Their ability to sell so well to a readership that a destitute Freneau, late in life, described as a public who "hate the bard, and spurn his rhymes"[30] suggests that slave narrative had more in common with American tastes than one would believe, including its lukewarm stance on poetry. In this sense, the successes of these writings by ex-slaves function in a manner similar to novels, which as Jane Thompkins wrote, "show what a text had *in common* with other texts. For a novel's impact on the culture at large depends not on its escape from the formulaic and derivative, but on its tapping into a storehouse of commonly held assumptions, reproducing what is already there

29　David W. Blight, "Introduction," in Frederick Douglass, *Narrative of the Life of Frederick Douglass, An American Slave, Written by Himself* (Boston: Bedford, 1993), 16.
30　Philip Freneau, "To a New England Poet," *The Last Poems of Philip Freneau*, ed. Lewis Leary (New Brunswick: Rutgers University Press, 1945), 112.

in a typical form. The text that becomes exceptional in the sense of reaching an exceptionally large audience does so not because of its departure from the ordinary and conventional, but through its embrace of what is most widely shared."[31]

After Phillis Wheatley the next major African-American writer—the tradition's second idea—would stake his reputation and set his ambition within the genre of the new boss, creative prose. Frederick Douglass's subsequent encounters with poetry would occur within his prose, his conflicts with genre would occur in a near-reverse fashion to Wheatley. Further, Douglass wrote his *Narrative*, as all slaves did, after slavery. The genre of the slave narrative holds as one of its muted precepts that the author is not a slave. Slave narratives, teleological in their narrative impetus, move of course from slavery to freedom, with the final word—"freedom"—falling with the heaviness, and inevitability, of rhyme. The days of saying something without saying it through the arabesque of poetic form were all but over. That old and daedal exercise of poetic fancy stood no chance against the pragmatic authority of prose and plot.

Frederick Douglass was not only writing during a time when his freedom was under threat (he left the country for a substantial period of time when the *Narrative* was originally published to avoid capture, he was still a runagate). Douglass also wrote his first *Narrative* within a crucible of generic crisis. He was a writer troubled to his core by an antagonistic dynamic between the prosaic and the poetic. This trouble made his prose as much about the poetic as about the narrative that made him the most famous

---

31   Jane Thompkins, *Sensational Designs: The Cultural Work of American Fiction, 1790–1860* (New York: Oxford, 1985), xvi.

ex-slave the world would know. If we look once again at the 1845 text, we will discover that Douglass's *Narrative* avoids slave verse with the same determination with which it searches for authorial control, personal freedom, and a substantiated masculinity.

Slave verse, he makes clear, is a discourse and sign antagonistic to writing. This is why, while this early chapter (and it must occur early, must it not?) is an essential component in the creation of the narrative voice and while it is in actuality the most unique defense of poetry in American letters, it can neither emboss nor in the end endorse the visual imprint of its subject matter. The second chapter of the Douglass *Narrative* is a defense of a new lyrical form's existence that provides no textual space for that lyrical form to appear. Why, then, does Douglass mention slave verse at all? Instead of tacking on a parody of an established Southern church hymn onto the end of his *Narrative* as he does with the appearance of "A Parody" which appears in the "Appendix" of the *Narrative*), why doesn't Douglass simply reproduce the verses of his "brethren in bonds"—especially since he goes to such elegant and entreating lengths to describe their power?

One reason is that Douglass must turn to slave verse in order to authenticate his intimate knowledge of the experience of slavery, but he must also disavow it in order to maintain his authorial stature as a free and articulate individual. To this end, Douglass uses the lyric expression of slave verse as a counterpoint to the ethnographic material of the *Narrative* itself.

Instead of allegorizing his remembrance of slave verse into a moment prescriptive of *all* Blacks, Douglass insists that he was "not the only slave in the world." Yet his implicit and very subdued association of freedom with poetic comprehension and the teary, apostrophic rendering of his reaction as he writes his "own lines" brings into question the dynamic between an emergent African-American literature, verse, and the discovery of freedom as it pertains to human experience.

I will show that the slave songs in this instance of the *Narrative* (which we must remember is a written summation, a form of criticism and elaboration, which occurs *before* the slave songs were collected in book form) are completely enclosed within Douglass's construction of his interiority. It is Douglass and not the *Narrative* that contains the meaning of slave verse; he gives us the *effect* of the lyric instead of the lyric itself. By sublimating verse within the body of his narrative, Douglass foreshadows how African-American letters will come to view and sublimate lyric experience with the larger prosaic phenomenon.[32] Douglass turns his prose into a generic filter: a conventional mediator of a textually inchoate past. As slaves were denied their right to a historical apparatus and hence a genealogy of agency and artistry, the narrative becomes for the author all at once history, genealogy, and authenticated fact. Under these circumstances, what is historical for the slave must also be tangible; in other words ex-slaves were engaged in the formation of a generic object that could be enjoyed and employed by a readership that wished to

---

32 My use of the psychoanalytical term "sublimation" is in keeping more with Harry Stack Sullivan's sense of it than with Freud's. Sublimation, in Sullivan's words, refers to an "unwitting substitution, for a behavior pattern which causes anxiety or collides with the self-system, of a socially more appropriate activity pattern which satisfies part of the motivational system that caused trouble." Thus, here I am using "sublimation" to indicate the psyche's socially acceptable resolution to an anxiety-producing situation rather than to a natural response of the defense mechanism. Cf., F. Barton Evans, III, *Harry Stack Sullivan: Interpersonal Theory and Psychotherapy* (London: Routledge, 1996), 99.

feign the inclusion of these products, these texts, into an articulate, tangible, and thus verifiable America.

Russ Castronovo has read these prose texts as such, "Autobiographies and fictions by ex-slaves form a necessary supplement to the corpus of foundational documents and legacies that define and constitute national narrative," yet then notes a destabilizing aspect to their narrativity. "But these supplements," he argues "hardly shore up that narrative." What Castronovo views as a drama of "discursive passing," meaning a set of "interstices between ex-slave writings and national narrative," I read instead as a drama between the hyphen of "ex" and "slave."[33] If we follow Douglass's argument to its fruition, we find that from "slave" to "ex-slave" there is a distillation of the language of spontaneous verse unrealized as text to the hard font, page, and print of the emancipatory narrative. The gap between the two modes of being in the world takes on for the emancipated writer an allegorical impetus, whereby the rather fixed nature of slavery may produce idealizations or abstractions of the sign of slavery. The ex-slave narrative, then, writing on slave song, mediates upon an allegory of the poetry of American antebellum entrapment in order to fashion a vital difference of constitution for the liberated writer. Perhaps as true to its etymology as can be attained, an instance like Douglass's writing *over* slave songs is a case of allegory as the other (liberated, text-based, prose-fashioned, and historically conjectured) speaking.

We discover in his discussion of slave verse Douglass's first moment of authority, where his attempt to master a narrative-of-the-self yields its priority to the authority of a critical voice:

---

33   Russ Castronovo, *Fathering the Nation: American Genealogies of Slavery and Freedom* (Berkeley: University of California Press, 1995), 199.

a critical voice that writes masterfully on (in both senses of the word) the lyric. Unlike the lines from Cowper and Whittier fluidly embedded within Douglass's prose, the lyrics sung by slaves had no conventional textual form that would allow Douglass to recuperate them whole-cloth in prose.[34] The major poets of the era carry within their texts a cultural if not material value that Douglass's re-quoting, and textual embedding, then turns seamlessly into emotional paraphrase. Douglass learns to use American poetry as an already-formed outlet for emotion. Thus, and by example, another major moment of pathos in the *Narrative* takes the loss of Douglass's mistress Lucretia, the overturning of all of the property to "the hands of strangers—strangers who had had nothing to do with accumulating it," and the subsequent exile by these strangers of Douglass's elemental grandmother "who was now very old, having outlived [her] old master and all his children, having seen the beginning and end of all of them . . . her frame already racked with the pains of old age complete helplessness fast stealing over her once active limbs, they took her to the woods [and] built her a little hut . . . thus virtually welcoming her to die!" Douglass, here, prescribes not the *feeling* of poetry, but rather the *text* of Whittier to paraphrase (or more I should say supplement, as the paraphrase occurs with the object that would have been paraphrased). Douglass writes,

> If my poor old grandmother now lives, she lives to suffer in utter loneliness; she lives to remember and mourn

34   A portion of Cowper's poem "Time Piece," from 1785, appears in chapter two, the slave-song chapter of the *Narrative*. Whitter's poem "The Farewell," a poem published in 1835, appears in chapter nine, and his "Clerical Oppressors," a poem published in 1836, appears in the "Appendix" of the *Narrative*.

over the loss of children, the loss of grandchildren, and the loss of great-grandchildren. They are, in the language of the slave's poet, Whittier—

> Gone, gone, sold and gone
> To rice swamp dank and lone,
> Where the slave-whip ceaseless swings,
> Where noisome insect stings,
> Where the fever-demon strews
> Poison with the falling dews,
> Where the sickly sunbeams glare
> Through the hot and misty air: —
>> Gone, gone, sold and gone
>> To the rice swamp dank and lone,
>> From Virginia hills and waters—
>> Woe is me, my stolen daughters!

The slave songs are a completely different matter, despite the fact that they provide—in artistic terms—more of a situated context for Douglass's genealogical lament than would have Whittier. Though the woe of the slave songs would perhaps have been an appropriate ode to Douglass's memorial sense of private loss, it lacked any sort of a retrievable signifier. As we read the second chapter of the *Narrative* we should never lose sight of the fact that the content is heavily descriptive and self-consciously distanced. "Description is *ancilla narrationis*, the ever-necessary, never-emancipated slave of narrative," wrote Gérard Genette. Douglass's language, his power of un-represented poetry, functions as a systemic replacement for something the reader must assume is already there. In other words, slave songs need not be quoted—if they are even quotable given their penchant for improvisation and revision—for their material even in prose re-capitulations provide all that is necessary: an interpretation of immediate effect. Slave songs are not important to Douglass for what they say or who they say them to, but rather for what they do and for whom. Again, Douglass is a visitor in prose to the changing portals of verse. Ultimately, what he takes in literate terms from within these contexts—an interpretive aspect of verse in context with the prosaic design of the self—is the marrow with which he constitutes himself. The rest, what verse that emanates as distant memory in the second chapter of the *Narrative*, we are encouraged to read simply as residue.

We find in later African-American prose texts such as *The Souls of Black Folk, Cane, Invisible Man, Dessa Rose,* and *Jazz,* that *the* culturally authenticating sign by which prose writers come to encode the particular nuances of a divided self is the brazenly anti-novelistic lyric. But the nineteenth century politics of authorship and of the emergent market of the book put Doug-lass's *Narrative* at great odds with a kind of lyric, slave verse, still uncollected at the time. This would be the case until the 1867 publishing of *Slave Songs of the United States.* However, even the setting of these verses to press would not alone substantiate them as a truth-based medium for language, something essential to the Douglass project, as evidenced by William Allen in his intro-duction to the collection.

> The difficulty experienced in attaining absolute correct-ness is greater than might be supposed by those who

have never tried the experiment, and we are far from claiming that we have made no mistakes . . . What may appear to be an incorrect rendering, is very likely to be a variation; for these variations are endless, and very entertaining and instructive.[35]

Though perhaps "entertaining and instructive" for an emergent post-Civil War readership, Douglass could not afford the possible "incorrect rendering" that served as an accompaniment to these verses that were, understandably, treated more as music than as poetry. Douglass's narrative worked from within an established genre, the ex-slave narrative, and to stray toward verse would have catapulted Douglass into what Ronald Radano called "an accumulation of imagined otherness" in which "the spirituals, newly recorded as text, marked the outer limits of a racialized unknown existing beyond its makers' own access. Eventually, the inaccessibility of the spiritual would become in itself a fetish object that generated desperate attempts of recovery and control."[36] Instead of drifting toward an irretrievable signifier, the perceived unintelligibility of the spirituals, Douglass had to set his writing within a bound context of perceived and confirmed realities. Those things that function as a realist text does when it supposes an image of a world similar to what Jonathan Culler terms as set "into relation with a type of discourse or model which is, already, in some sense, natural *and* legible."[37]

35   William Francis Allen, Charles Pickford Ware, and Lucy McKin Garrison, eds., *Slave Songs of the United States* (New York: A. Simpson & Co., 1867), iv.
36   Ronald Radano, *Lying Up a Nation: Race and Black Music* (Chicago: University of Chicago Press, 2003), 184.
37   Jonathan Culler, *Structuralist Poetics: Structuralism, Linguistics, and the Study of Literature* (New York: Routledge, 1975), 138.

This is why we hear in Douglass's description of slave verse a fidgety set of contrasts between unauthored, unbound, and exoticized slave lyrics, and hardbound books of discursive prose. Douglass notes:

> I have sometimes thought the mere hearing of those songs would impress some minds with the horrible character of slavery, than the reading of whole volumes of philosophy on the subject could do.

What Douglass has "sometimes thought" he knows cannot and will not occur; it is a whimsical desire. And by pitting the two against one another—the fragmentary, unbound songs of slaves and the "whole volumes of philosophy"—Douglass only calls attention to the fact that he did not think that the reproduction of slave verse would do for him or his cause what the book and his *Narrative* could do. Given that I devote most of my energy to poetry, in particular to the writing of poetry, I sense it wherever it is buried in prose. There are few more startling examples of this in the modern ages of literature than in Fredrick Douglass's *Narrative*, where Douglass must come to know this lyric self as a different self, written as a lyric past, and then kill it.

Gordon Tesky, in his book on Renaissance poetics and allegorical interpretation, *Allegory and Violence*, discusses this process of objectifying the self as other and then annihilating it in terms of consumption.

> Every body wants to include the universe inside it; but every body, it seeing others like it, knows that these others desire the same. They represent alternate worlds. The

existence of other bodies therefore represents the most serious impediment to the hope of including the world in the self. The body of the other must therefore be annihilated in the only way possible: by devouring it.[38]

Understandably, then, Douglass's disavowing of the lyric yields a physiological response. Or so he writes, "The mere recurrence to those songs, even now, afflicts me; and while I am writing these lines, an expression of feeling has already found my cheek." In writing, he mimics the idea of consumption, the taking of something into the body. The body has no suitable outlet for such poetic memory, there is no *port esquiline* for Douglass. The body of narrative converts the lyric into tears that fall on the prosaic hand that still, as though determined to refute the pathos of the lyric, insists in converting it into prose.

Douglass is traversing the terrain of the hyphen. This chapter displays a lyricism unmatched throughout the rest of the *Narrative*. Yearning for authorship being too close to verse, Douglass bears the full burden of representation, of poetic interpretation and familiarity with both sides of the hyphen. Douglass calms the lyric moment by seeking refuge in a larger realm of knowledge, and concludes his chapter with a poetics of exile.

The singing of a man cast away upon a desolate island might be as appropriately considered as evidence of contentment and happiness, as the singing of a slave; the songs of the one and of the other are prompted by the same emotion.

---

38   Gordon Tesky, *Allegory and Violence* (Ithaca: Cornell University Press, 1996), 8.

As the elegance of Robert Lowell's poetry carried at its heart a deep neurosis muscled by an inherited and geographically sensitive past then we can read Lowell as arguably the heir of Frederick Douglass, who fought the burden of being authentic, fought back the blows of his master, and fought the familial ghosts of poetry. Lowell, all poet, could not find freedom in meter and so turned his poetry inside out and had it confess his sins. Douglass, all prose, lacked the necessary belief that verse could spell his civility and break him free from the confinement of the pre-Enlightened slave.

While Douglass's commentary on slave songs cannot be fairly classified as poetic criticism, he nevertheless outlines a particular way of reading them that I wish to discuss.

> I did not, when a slave, understand the deep meaning of those rude and apparently incoherent songs. I was myself within the circle; so I neither saw nor heard as those without might see and hear. They told a tale of woe which was then altogether beyond my feeble comprehension; they were tones loud, long, and deep; they breathed the prayer and complaint of souls boiling over with the bitterest anguish. Every tone was a testimony against slavery, and a prayer to God for deliverance from chains. The hearing of those wild notes always depressed my spirit, and filled me with ineffable sadness. I have frequently found myself in tears while hearing them. The mere recurrence to those songs, even now, afflicts me; and while I am writing these lines, an expression of feeling has already found its way down my cheek. To those

songs I trace my first glimmering conception of the de-humanizing character of slavery. I can never get rid of that conception. Those songs still follow me, to my hatred of slavery, and quicken my sympathies for my brethren in bonds.

Why did Douglass believe that it was only after he had achieved his freedom—a stylized articulated freedom—that he could comprehend the songs of his "brethren in bonds"? Is Douglass's escape from his bondage a novelistic escape, his path to freedom prose-ridden? Douglass's *Narrative* functions both as a slave narrative and as a *Bildungsroman*. Its episodic derailments of slavery's effect on his human development encourage a teleological reading of Douglass's progression from slave to—as he would cite the difference—man. Denied the opportunity to be taught to read, he teaches himself: "From that moment I understood the pathway from slavery to freedom. It was just what I wanted, and I got it at a time when I the least expected it . . . Though conscious of the difficulty of learning without a teacher, I set out with high hope, and a fixed purpose, at whatever cost of trouble to learn to read." Faced with ritualistic submission, he fights back, fights the ritual off: "My long-crushed spirit rose, cowardice departed, bold defiance took its place; and I now resolved that, however long I might remain a slave in form, the day had passed forever when I could be a slave in fact. I did not hesitate to let it be known of me, that the white man who expected to succeed in whipping, must also succeed in killing me." Douglass, amidst the difficult work of substantiating his humanness within a world attempting to counteract his existence, configured writing and resistance as the sun and moon of his new days as a self-realized individual. As is well known, the arbiters of American slave society took the legality of both the crafted word and the self-directed hand from their captives with a desperate and paranoid fervor. Douglass's incorporation of both literacy and defensive-combativeness serve at once as the plied trade of the newly liberated (in that one has taken steps to free one's self) and as the metaphorical preamble to succeeding African-American texts (the developing genre of slave narratives, the African-American novel, and—later—the metacriticism that sought to allegorize these movements toward self-ascribed freedom as a larger circumscription for the reading of black texts).

Douglass clearly felt as though his life as a slave was burdened by a contradiction: he knew that he existed, but as a slave he was treated as though he did not exist. Of course, to say that one is treated as though one does not exist does not mean that one is literally not seen. Ellison's symptoms for his protagonist's invisibility included a failure to treat him as a complex set of occasions, hence when he quipped that "people fail to see" him, he meant that what they saw were their own complex set of assumptions. The coda, then, for *Invisible Man*, "Who knows, but that on the lower frequencies, I speak for you?" qualifies as the protagonist's self-inflicted desire not to be heard, but to have the *option* of being heard. The question is both literal and rhetorical—and may be answered or may not. To suggest that that desire is merely to be heard yokes the process of self-definition within a troubling binary of black absence versus presence. Freedom, in other words, is neither the ability to speak nor to be heard (that still is to reduce the issue to a matter of physiology, of tissue). Freedom is at the heart of both philosophy and verse as it is a conjecture of the possibility of a new way of experiencing something that already exists. Lyric poetry presumes an audience and in that very presumption asks of its audience to redress the schism between reader and lyric.

Herein lies the pitfall in articulating something new: that there is the possibility of not being understood, if even heard at all. If one is not understood one may remain unheard *but the idea still is realized.* It is still there. Freedom, then, does not come from an exterior source—there is no "Other" that grants freedom. Freedom is understood within the vessel of the individual, not clasped within reasoning. It is willed into existence. So we find that as Douglass began to do what was forbidden—reading and resisting—he found himself engaged in action beyond his circumstance: slaves neither read nor resist. Yet, as Douglass notes, there was nothing "unnatural" in his actions, nothing catastrophic. To deny one's self-freedom from that point on would be an invocation of what existentialists would cite as anguish: a decision not to decide.

This deliberation between two disparate forms, one objective and the other subjective, was not an innate situation for Douglass. Authorship came only with its necessary distance from the confines of slavery. Douglass was what Robert B. Stepto considered an "articulate survivor." As part of what he considers an "ascent narrative," Stepto argues that a "classic ascent narrative launches an 'enslaved' and semiliterate figure on a ritualized journey to a symbolic North." Adhering rigorously to an African-Americanist formalism, Stepto finds that freedom comes from a comprehension and subsequent manipulation of the polyphony of signs that mark a narrative. Freedom he qualifies as "the sense that he or she has granted sufficient literacy to assume the mantle of an articulate survivor." Stepto continues: "As the phrase 'articulate survivor' suggests, the hero or heroine of an ascent narrative must be willing to forsake familial or communal postures in the narrative's most oppressive social structure for a new posture in the least oppressive environment—at best one of solitude; at worst, one of alienation."[39]

Douglass's prose acts almost as a pardon for each verse's repetitiveness, its apparent unintelligibility, its orality and insistence on minor changes on the third and seventh of the pentatonic scale (what are commonly referred to as "blue notes"). Separated from the earliest poetry and apart from its immediate context, Douglass, now as an articulate survivor, can incorporate its tragic lines within the larger scope of his own paragraphs. Essential in this template is a form of African-American literary "progress" that is often overlooked: the qualitative movement from verse to prose. Verse is the stuff of emotion and the humors, prose that of the calmer side of intellectual exploration. Verse is a strange engine for Douglass as it permeates the parameters of his freedom, kinship, and literary acumen as much as his encounters with more immediate traumas. In his appendix to the *Narrative* Douglass concludes with a verse he calls a "portrait of the religion of the South"; a religion where, as he notes, "the slave auctioneer's bell and the church-going bell chime in with each other, and the bitter cries of the heart-broken slave are drown in the religious shouts of his pious master. Revivals

39   Robert Stepto, *From Behind the Veil: A Study of Afro-American Narrative* (Urbana: University of Illinois Press, 1979), 167.

of religion and revivals of the slave-trade go hand in hand to-gether. The slave prison and the church stand near each other." The poem, entitled "A Parody," I will quote here in its entirety.

A Parody

Come, saints and sinners, hear me tell
How pious priests whip Jack and Nell,
And women buy and children sell,
And preach all sinners down to hell,
    And sing of heavenly union.

They'll bleat and baa, dona like goats,
Gorge down black sheep, and strain at motes,
Array their backs in fine black coats,
Then seize their negroes by their throats,
    And choke for heavenly union.

They'll church you if you sip a dram,
And damn you if you steal a lamb;
Yet rob old Tony, Doll, and Sam,
Of human rights, and bread and ham;
    Kidnapper's heavenly union.

They'll loudly talk of Christ's reward,
And bind his image with a cord,
And scold, and swing the lash abhorred,
And sell their brother in the Lord
    To handcuffed heavenly union.

We wonder how such saints can sing,
Or praise the Lord upon the wing,
Who roar, and scold, and whip, and sting,
And to their slaves and mammon cling
  In guilty conscience union.

They'll raise tobacco, corn, and rye,
And drive, and thieve, and cheat, and lie,
And lay up treasures in the sky,
By making switch and cowskin fly,
  In hope of heavenly union.

A roaring, ranting, sleek man-thief,
Who lived on mutton, veal, and beef,
Yet never would afford relief
To needy, sable sons of grief,
  Was big with heavenly union.

"Love not the world," the preacher said,
And winked his eye, and shook his head;
He seized on Tom, and Dick, and Ned,
Cut short their meat, and clothes, and bread,
  Yet still loved heavenly union.

Another preacher whining spoke
Of One whose heart for sinners broke:
He tied old Nanny to an oak,
And drew blood at every stroke,
  And prayed for heavenly union.

Two others oped their iron jaws,
And waved their children-stealing paws;
There sat their children in gewgaws;
By stinting negroes' backs and maws,
  They kept up heavenly union.

All good from Jack another takes,
And entertains their flirts and rakes,
Who dress as sleek as glossy snakes,
And cram their mouths with sweetened cakes;
  And this goes down for union.

Is this part of the progression that has been internalized in African-American discourse? Did Douglass's stylized rumination upon a textually destabilizing past, a past of the hyphen, an ancient past full of Africa, anticipate teleologically his reproduction of Whittier and Cowper and then his demonstration of a mastery of the reproduction by way of parody? This is the progression of poetic forms in the book. The question is a dangerous one, for to answer in the affirmative is to imply that Douglass valued one manner of verse to another. I am neither prepared nor interested in making such a claim. Of far more value is to note *how* Douglass uses verse in both instances, and what that encounter premises for our past as well as our future as it pertains to the poetic spirit of America. We have already seen that it is after he has conceived of himself as free that Douglass feels at ease providing an exegesis of early African-American verse. He came to recognize these as his "first glimmering conception" of a state of non-being he once shared with the poet—whomever that poet may be. Douglass is an outsider, and from this enabling periphery he becomes a critic. Though aside from the distich

> I am going away to the Great House Farm!
> O, yea! O yea! O!

there are no remnants of the singing so essential to Douglass's renewal but for his own words. With "A Parody" we find instead that Douglass is an arbiter. He speaks as an insider, using the same language of authentication that was used by William Lloyd Garrison in his "Preface" to the *Narrative*. Stepto sees this as an inversion of roles:

> The poem is strong and imbued with considerable irony, but what we must appreciate here is the effect of the white Northerner's poem conjoined with Douglass's *Authentication* of the poem. The tables are clearly reversed: Douglass has not only controlled his personal history, but also fulfilled the prophecy suggested by his implicit authentication of Garrison's "Preface" by explicitly authenticating what is conventionally a white Northerner's validating text.[40]

Yet if Douglass's authenticating gloss of the visible poem grants him ultimate presence within and throughout his own text, then his critical gloss of the invisible slave songs provides him with an equivalent measure of "authenticity" and presence through his exegetical replacement of one level of meaning for another.

40　Stepto, *From Behind the Veil*, 26.

Douglass perhaps sensed somewhere in his writing of the *Narrative* that he was asked to translate (or perhaps, justify) a larger epic: the allegorical text of the New World, in which the "brethren in bonds" play the roles of allegorical figures who do not live singularly, but rather instruct. The clergyman Ephraim Peabody wrote a review of the ex-slave narratives of Douglass, William Wells Brown, and Josiah Henson in 1849 that spelled out the emergence of a new genre, "America has the mournful honor of adding a new department to the literature of civilization—the autobiographies of escaped slaves" (though one would be right to question this "mournful honor" was solely American).[41] Yet shortly thereafter, as Peabody's review continues to trumpet what has, sadly yet marvelously, arrived, he is writing more and more of older forms, and genres further from the narrative. First, Peabody appraises and then gives to the narrative a pictorial quality: "We place these volumes without hesitation among the most remarkable productions of the age—remarkable as being pictures of slavery by the slave." This quality of the "remarkable" is presented as a naturalized praxis outside of the bounds of its text: "not less remarkable as a vivid exhibition of the force and working of the native love of freedom in the individual mind." It is not "the individual mind" however, which provides for this reviewer the foundation for the narrative's strength. In fact, the review sets up the uniqueness of the narrative in order to privilege its poetic resonance; as a reminder of the great allegorical Homeric texts from which the literacy of the Westernized individual grounds

---

41   Ephraim Peadody, "Narratives of Fugitive Slaves," *Christian Examiner* 47 (July 1849): 61–93, quoted in *The Slave's Narrative*, eds. Charles T. Davis and Henry Louis Gates, Jr. (New York: Oxford University Press, 1991), 19.

its sourcing. The power of Douglass's *Narrative* comes precisely at the level in which it is considered an originary allegorical text, one which functions as an *Iliad* or *Odyssey*.

> There are those who fear lest the elements of poetry and romance should fade out of the tame and monotonous social life of modern times. There is no danger of it while there are any slaves left to seek for freedom, and to tell of their efforts to obtain it. There is that in the lives of men who have sufficient force of mind and heart to enable them to struggle up from hopeless bondage to the position of freemen, beside which the ordinary characters of romance are dull and tame. They encounter a whole Iliad of woes, not in plundering and enslaving others, but in recovering themselves those rights of which they have been deprived from birth. Or if the Iliad should be thought not to present a parallel case, we know not where one who wished to write a modern Odyssey could find better subject than in the adventures of a fugitive slave.[42]

Peabody, a Bowdoin graduate and part of the Boston clergy, sought for Douglass a life outside of "the antislavery cause" from which he had learned "the 'withering and scorching' eloquence with which American speeches seem so to abound." Are we to assume that his aversion to what he considered the propagandizing of art was for the sake of truth? "When men are profoundly in earnest," Peabody admonished, "they are not apt to be extravagant." Peabody is never frank with us as to where exactly the

---

42   Ibid.

extravagance in Douglass's *Narrative* resides. But given his praise of Douglass's "personal knowledge of slavery" and his parable of the merchant failing in his attempt to talk politics and losing his extravagance when engaged by "some enterprise which he really has deeply at heart"[43] we are to infer that it is Douglass's political asides. Peabody, somewhat in his defense, is attempting to praise Douglass's work for being, well, "Literature" (capitals intended) and views its original contribution to be where and how Douglass writes about slavery. Yet, the reductive tenor of his argument is still too pungent to swallow. For not only should Douglass, then, write intimately about slavery; but that very subject is configured in its entirety to contain all "the elements of poetry." What could be mis-read as an "elevation" of subject and content, I want to make clear is in actuality a reduction. To identify the black body as an object inseparable from poetry itself, as proves to be the case in the consideration of slave poet and slave verse, unintentionally sabotages the artist's ability to change, and the artist's ability to be complex. An entire people who contain poetry a priori contain the world inside of them, and lack reflection. There is accordingly no balance between world and subject, the very striving and necessary desire of the Romantics. The black body then is un-reflective, like the most beautiful statue, it is always its art, even beforehand (before written) when encased in its block of marble.

While it may seem strange that Phillis Wheatley needed her poetry authenticated and then after suffered criticism that her work was not poetry but imitation, while Frederick Douglass needed the content of his narrative authenticated and then suffered praise that his narrative was poetry, we should take this as the constant destabilization of genres that black writing both endures

---

43   Ibid., 25.

and enables. Without fail, genres have entered the Western world with the mass expulsion or subjugation of people of African descent. That the American novel, the ex-slave narrative, and lyric poem all situate their flourishing during the antebellum period leaves us to ponder what type of meaning then does the black writer place on each genre; and most importantly, on poetry, which has escaped our view as a genre of particular power and poignancy during this era largely due to the wild popularity of the narratives. The African-American poets of the nineteenth century instead became the "Invisible Poets" of the century, and faded out of view. Douglass's prose, however, stages a profound and instigating drama between the writer of prose and the sounds of verse. His writing on the slave songs seems to anticipate Peabody's collapse of slavery and poetry into one self-satisfying whole.

The invisible text is made visible, but as the ossification of a genre separate from poetry. Slave verse comes to matter as an appendage to both freedom and politics in becoming part of the ex-slave narrative's *raison de différence* and likewise an able text within the Abolitionist cause. At this point one may surmise that Douglass "employs writing to alter the very way in which Americans hear slave sound. Through the power of a masterful literary style, Douglass challenges the minstrel theme of the happy 'Sambo' and makes palpable and nearly audible the anguished resonances of slave singing. In this instance, Douglass uses text to amplify and to erase. Turning up the volume of slavery's horrors, he inscribes another, more oppositional view that prefigures W. E. B. Du Bois's image of the 'sorrow songs.'"[44] Yet what is amplified and what erased? If slave singing (which is slave verse)

44   Ronald Radano, "Denoting Difference: The Writing of the Slave Spirituals," *Critical Inquiry* 22:3 (1996): 507.

is retained or recovered through a "difference" it is one that marks the consumption of African-American verse by prose. Prose authenticates what it devours: the ineffable qualities of anonymous lyrics governed by the phoneme, some poignant admixture itself of West African and American airs.

For Douglass's *Narrative*, the notion of writerly critique both begins and concludes with verse. The inaugural encounter is "glimmering conception," inescapable and—like the verses themselves—incremental under the guise of repetition. Douglass, in a near Gothic thrall, admits, "I can never get rid of that conception. Those songs still follow me, to deepen my hatred of slavery, and quicken my sympathies for my brethren in bonds." The final encounter is with a derivative, British ballad that functions within the *Narrative* as an enabling critique of the genre of slave narratives themselves. Yet this progression (and it is to be read as a progression, as opposed to the revolving door epilogue of *Invisible Man*) must still be recognized as well as literary submission of the oral genre to the demands of prose. African-American verse is left to suffer an ontological rupture, bifurcating into a manichean split between prose and verse. Abdul R. JanMohamed argues along colonialist lines that

> The dominant model of power- and interest-relations in all colonial societies is the manichean opposition between the putative superiority of the European and the supposed inferiority of the native. This axis in turn provides the central feature of the colonialist cognitive framework and colonialist literary representation: the manichean allegory—a field of diverse yet interchange-

able oppositions between white and black, good and evil, superiority and inferiority, civilization and savagery, intelligence and emotion, rationality and sensuality, self and Other, subject and object.[45]

Thus, one finds that as much as Douglass cites his own freedom through literacy as a profound form of human being amidst hostility toward his existence, he likewise necessarily cites slave verse—wild, and invisible (meaning still uncollected, still oral)—as part of what was once his state of not-being. Unlike "A Parody" Douglass's critique of slavery is substitutional as opposed to supplemental. For Douglass's narrative, freedom's *written* tale needed to be authenticated as real material and only prose would have been profitable enough to fashion such a claim.

The space to form a substitutional critique is formed by Douglass to suit political ends more than aesthetic ones. We gather from his remarks in chapter two that he was stirred more by the slave song than by any other writing. Though significantly moved by verse and obsessed with the power of the pen, he was not a poet; and, though I take great liberty here, one supposes that that vocation would not have served Douglass as well given his ambition and vaguely existentialist principles. Thus, though the habit in African-American literary study is to conflict writing with orality, perhaps African-American literary study should as well conflict writing with writing. The blanketing of the act of writing as triumphant, the modes of orality as retentive, is a

---

45   Abdul R. JanMohamed, "The Economy of Manichean Allegory: The Function of Racial Difference in Colonialist Literature," in *Race, Writing and Difference*, ed. Henry Louis Gates, Jr. (Chicago: The University of Chicago Press, 1986), 82.

reflex of prose-determined thinking; and, if anything, we should recognize that "African-American literature" is a metonym for prose. For the most part, its canonical narratives and theoretical studies implement an early use of lyrical material later subsumed by, and for, prose models for comprehending the self and the texts in question. The implication is that the spontaneous evanescence of lyric verse is but a minor part of the hardened form of African-American reality: which is prosaic.

Douglass understood the climate in which he wrote perhaps as well as anyone who lived in his day; one merely need his three autobiographies to ascertain this. Hence, his exegesis of slave verse formulated a discovery, an inauguration, and a schematic. Where the uncollected poets, where Jupiter Hammon and Phillis Wheatley, where George Moses Horton had failed, Douglass would not. The anonymous slave verses were to become ossified as musical notation and stage performance, the earlier written work of the aforementioned poets risked quickly evaporating into ethnographic footnotes. Consequently, Douglass's analysis is paradoxically redemptive (a recollection of poetic language possibly lost or forgotten) and destructive (as it displaces the aesthetic subjectivity of that language with its dominating affect). What was written allegorizes what was, or more precisely, over what was said by a Douglass who, in the dually responsible role of historian and critic, must register "the shock at the epicenter of his work," which is what Benjamin saw in Baudelaire, who is referred to by some as the first modern poet of the world. Freedom, we find from Douglass's ambiguities, is not teleological process, as neither a full embrace nor a full rejection of poetry can serve this project of freeing the self on its own. Prose has, however, come to institute itself as a function of representations viewed as "a historically peculiar social formation . . . inevitable, natural, a necessary function of the 'real' itself."[46] The reinvestigation of prosaic moments where an utter investment in the poetic marks its emanation is upon us. The teleological is giving way to the chiasmus. The straight line of the hyphen revealing thus its jagged terrain and ruts. As Geoffrey Hartman has remarked

> This chiasmus of hope and catastrophe is what saves hope from being unmasked as only catastrophe: as an illusion or unsatisfied movement of desire that wrecks everything. The foundation of hope becomes remembrance; which confirms the function, even the duty of historian and critic. To recall the past is a political act: a "recherche" that involves us with images of peculiar power, images that may constrain us to identify with them, that claim the "*weak* Messianic power" in us (Thesis 2). These images, split off from their fixed location in history, undo concepts of homogeneous time, flash up into or reconstitute the present.[47]

The "chiasmus of hope and catastrophe" reveals the necessary deferral of hope in order to prevent the possibility of total catastrophe. Both must co-exist together, like birth and death, or that pungently metaphorical image of the serpent devouring its tail.

46   James H. Kavanah, "Ideology," in *Critical Terms for Literary Study*, ed. Frank Lentricchia and Thomas McLaughlin (Chicago: The University of Chicago Press, 1990), 310.
47   Geoffrey Hartman, *Criticism and the Wilderness* (New Haven: Yale University Press, 1980), 78.

Hope, a dream-state, must remain deferred to hold off catastrophe, a threatening presence that hints at itself in all the ruins of modern time. For African-American literature this paradigmatic X is not the ruins of antiquity that contend present and past, but the very presence of Black difference on this hemisphere; the ossified hyphen, its own toppled pillar in ruin. These spirituals, as practical as they were poignant, seized their "peculiar power" (to borrow from Hartman) from their repetitive nature. Hence, in formal terms, the past functioned as a palimpsest of poetic intent: they repeat along lines both vertical and horizontal. To recall a line, in other words, to make a refrain, is to revisit the texture of the previous line. It is to make the poem perform itself again. The lyric poem insists upon itself. This is the horizontal tenure of repetition as a replacement of a prior utterance. This same repetition argues for its vertical musculature when the poems become reified as text. Any spiritual will look on paper like perfunctoriness in bed with itself. But this is a challenge, as Benjamin saw it, to homogeneous time.

The power of interpretation is perennially part of the supposed progression toward freedom and the establishment of a self-selected identity. Were, then, Douglass's observations on slave verse indicative of a manichean dichotomy between the free writer and the enslaved poet? And if freedom substantiates a sustainable writerly consciousness, the manifestations of which subsequently appearing nearly exclusively as prose narratives, then what does this say for the enslaved singers, those whose songs were soon to become so fashionable yet their names long ago erased to condemn the innocent?

III *an early epilogue*

In all three of his autobiographies Douglass gives fundamental importance to his fight with Covey the slave breaker. In the *Narrative* he writes,

> The battle with Mr. Covey was the turning-point in my career as a slave. It rekindled the few expiring embers of freedom, and revived within me a sense of my own manhood. It recalled the departed self-confidence, and inspired me again with a determination to be free . . . I felt as I had never felt before. It was a glorious resurrection, from the tomb of slavery, to the heaven of freedom. My long-crushed spirit rose, cowardice departed, bold deviance took its place; and I now resolved that, however long I might remain a slave in form, the day had passed forever when I could be a slave in fact.

Instead of returning to the numerous critical views of the significance of this scene—which range from (but are not limited to) Douglass's construction of his own identity as a free man despite his continued status as a slave, the philosophical nuances of this position, the allegorical implications of the fight itself, or the divisions between ideas of freedom and gender caused by Douglass's devotion to making his self-styled liberation one centering on manhood, instead of any of this—I will be turning our focus away from the episode itself and onto the two lines of verse that mark the very end of this episode. And consequently, we will return to the *Narrative* and revisit the first time that Douglass writes down this episode in order to take a closer look at the blank space where those two lines of verse would, in subsequent versions of Douglass's autobiography, later appear.

The Narrative is the only of the three Douglass autobiographies that does not conclude the Covey-fight episode with two lines from Byron. The presence of Byron then is an addition to the autobiography. What, we should ask, do these lines add? Why do they appear in the second and third versions of Douglass's autobiography, by which time he was quite famous? What function do these lines have?

> Hereditary bondsmen, know ye not
> Who would be free, themselves must strike the first blow?

From *Childe Harold's Pilgrimage*, Canto II, stanza lxxvi, they are arguably the most famous lines in the poem. Perhaps Douglass found them incredibly apropos, after having read them. He would have been reading a poet who, somewhat like he, woke one morning and discovered that he was incredibly famous. The lines were a cultural lingua franca among his contemporaries. This was the case to such an extent that Martin Delany's black periodical *The Mystery*, which was published out of Pittsburgh from 1843 to 1848, used the lines as an epigraph. The complex relationship between and intertwined legacies of Douglass and Delany, the role the abolitionist William Llord Garrison played in it, and the story of the path from Pittsburgh and Delany's black radical *The Mystery* to Rochester and Douglass's abolitionist *North Star* is a tale for another space.[48] Suffice it to say

---

48   Cf. Robert S. Levine, *Martin Delany, Frederick Douglass and the Politics of Representative Identity* (Chapel Hill: The University of North Carolina Press, 1997).

that a regular reader of *The Mystery* would be well acquainted with those lines.

Nevertheless, we can imagine the intervention of poetry into the text as being private, allusive, domestic, fraternal, random, calculated, perhaps market-driven. We do not know. But without these lines, the chapter on Covey (chapter XXI) in *My Bondage and My Freedom*, for example, would end: "I had made up my mind to do him serious damage, if he ever again attempted to lay his violent hands on me." The difference in the chapter's conclusion without the verse is the notable lingering residue of violence, Douglass dangling from his sentence as the direct object, the singular objective pronoun, the experience closed linguistically yet open rhetorically and psychologically like a gaping wound still without its suture of final anodynic mediation. The verse is that suture. It fashions a reader, including her or him without didactic direction into the imagination of the creation (you know these lines, reader, and they take you where they take you—note that the literal understanding of these lines is that the Greeks should fight as the Spanish did, but to the English these lines were always allegorical). Verse here is an intervention, a mediator, but not due to its content, but rather due to the fact that it is first and foremost poetic material and as such signifies in ways that the prose of the ex-slave narrative could not. Bryon's lyrics are the textual segue between chapter (entitled "My Last Flogging," the last statement of which being "if he ever again attempted to lay his violent hands on me") and the title/subtitle of the succeeding chapter, "My Life as a Freeman"/"Liberty Attained." It is precisely the lyric's ability to behave as an adjective in this instance by means of its fragmentation of the narrative experience, which allows the narrative to become "forgetful" and to start therefore again, ever so slightly outside of the time in which it was originally rendered. Understood in this light, the fact that chapter XXII begins what seems merely an aside to move the narrative forward—"There is no necessity for any extended notice of the incidents of this part of my life. There is nothing very striking or peculiar about my life as a freeman, when viewed apart from my life as a slave"—reveals itself instead to be the inevitable effect of the palimsestic significance of its generic aftermath.

We should turn from Chapter XXI of *My Bondage and My Freedom* to the "Introduction," for there we find these two lines from Byron again. They are repeated (or cribbed) in the introduction by James M'Cune Smith, whose pre-emptive quoting of Byron performs two acts: the first being that when we arrive at the two lines again when used by Douglass, the lines echo Smith's usage of them; the second being that the light of post-authorship—that moment by which we apply language that is not our own and make it ours—is dimmed. This is the paratextual shellgame of all introductions: despite their foregrounded nature they are always ancillary texts. Nevertheless, while it is possible that Douglass did get the line from Smith, it is just as possible that Smith took the line directly from Douglass. It is hard to believe that Smith would not have at the very least read the chapter of the battle with Covey. The history of reading attestations of slave narratives as necessary authentications would likely imply to many a reader an inauguration of the idea of the line by Smith. Yet I am less interested in the answer to this question and far more in the work it performs. For Smith the inclusion of Byron's lines are not to bridge the personal experience of an individual to an audience and slave to free author but rather to make a transatlantic appeal.

[H]is sojourn in England was more than a joy to Mr. Douglass. Like the platform at Nantucket, it awakened him to the consciousness of new powers that lay in him. From the pupilage of Garrisonism he rose to the dignity of a teacher and a thinker; his opinions on the broader aspects of the great American question were earnestly and incessantly sought, from various points of view, and he must, perforce, bestir himself to give suitable answer. With that prompt and truthful perception which has led their sisters in all ages of the world to gather at the feet and support the hands of the reformers, the gentle-women of England were foremost to encourage and strengthen him to carve out for himself a path fitted to his powers and energies, in the life-battle against slavery and caste to which he was pledged. And one stirring thought, inseparable from the British idea of the evangel of freedom, must have smote his ear from every side—

"Hereditary bondmen! know ye not
Who would be free, themselves must strike the blow?"

Smith intimates that Douglass is charged with an English abolitionist spirit now, an energy charged by the Byronic hero, or at least the Byronic heroic voice. Note the conclusion of Smith's evocation of the Byronic spirit with his referencing the American newspaper.

But also note that Smith maintains the metrical rigor of the second line: "Who would be free, themselves must strike the blow?" while Douglass added an extra syllable in the form of the rather pointed word "first": "Who would be free, themselves must strike the *first* blow?" This subsequently adds not only inauguration to the conception and to the possible action (perhaps a sign of the neophyte American not harkening back to the Greeks and Spanish?) but the spondaic end of the new hendecasyllabic line leaves an equal rhetorical and sonic charge between "first" and "blow." They vie now, always, for priority.

Further, the lines in question are not an unrhymed couplet, but instead the first two lines of a Spenserian stanza; one within a narrative poem of four cantos and four hundred and sixty one Spenserian stanzas. The reduction, then, to the distich should remind one of a poet reducing an idea to its particulars: Pound reigning in "At the Station of the Metro" to two lines from thirty, for instance. But, more immediately, we should recall Douglass himself when thinking of the songs he used to hear on the plantation, those lyrics he considered his "first glimmering conception of the dehumanizing affect of slavery." Given the possibility to replicate, insert, or quote any number of the panoply of lyrics from his "brethen in bonds," he gave us two. This twinning revision of the autobiographical English Romantic poem, and the endless strophes (endless because thus far unwritten) of the slave songs, the lyric of his people is the necessary next step in understanding Frederick Douglass. The lyric is the visual and representational matter that turns the screw of all conceptions of himself as ex-slave and free writer. Poetic quotation was certainly another method by which the individual was free and articulate (meaning speaking but also, in its Latinate sense, connected and flexible) with its culture and language, the self being fashioned not solely by the cultural value of knowing how to deploy poetry but by the authorial power of concision. Sonnets can become quatrains, terza rima a monostich, Spenserian stanzas can seem couplets, and prose—due to its inevitable limitations—can become the lyric, or the mind in search of the lyric, if only for two or four lines at a time.

THE BLUE CENTURY:
BRIEF NOTES ON TWENTIETH-CENTURY
AFRICAN-AMERICAN POETRY

Twentieth-century African-American poetry actually began in the last decade of the nineteenth century with the work of Paul Laurence Dunbar. While the poets and poems of the Harlem Renaissance can also stake a strong claim to this designation—due in large part to the dawn of the jazz age and a new consumer market for the black artist mainly by white patrons in the swelling urban centers of America—I would argue instead that it was the quiet turbulence of Dunbar's poems that form the start of twentieth-century African-American poetry. With *Oak and Ivy* (1893), *Majors and Minors* (1895), and *Lyrics of Lowly Life* (1896), Dunbar, born in Dayton, Ohio, created a poetics of duality. The titles alone of Dunbar's first two volumes of verse offer a manner by which to conceive of Dunbar's poetry as being riddled by a two-sided subjectivity, a play of needful contrasts: one and the other, this and that, not as canceling conceits but rather complementary parts of a whole; oak trees and ivy may form a forest, major and minors produce emotional tones in the musical progressions of scales, chords, and melodies. But then what of the third title? "Lyrics of lowly life" as a phrase not only eschews the simplistic balance of the first two titles, but it gives the sense of a weariness, indeed a fatigue that may be—given the words of the title—of a moral ("lowly life") or aesthetic ("lyrics") nature.

The bifurcated sensibility evident in the first two titles—a twinning that implies a separation of familiar entities—is the first major mode of African-American poetry in the twentieth century. Dunbar's poems were of two minds. There was the poet of the traditional English lyric, such as in "Ere Sleep Comes Down to Soothe the Weary Eyes":

> Ere sleep comes down to soothe the weary eyes,
>   Which all the day with ceaseless care have sought
> The magic gold which from the seeker flies[49]

But then there was the more lauded Dunbar: the poet of African-American rural speech, a dialect where the central personae would often have a sentimental eye on a simpler time (which would, given the chronology of the poems, inevitably be the antebellum period). For example, Dunbar's "When de Co'n Pone's Hot" utilizes the line "When yo' mammy says de blessin' / An' de co'n pone's hot" both as refrain and as calming respite from destabilizing moments ("When de worl' jes' stahts a-spinnin'"). Corn meal was commonly referred to as "corn pone" in Southern dialects and served as a primary staple for African-Americans during the antebellum era, Reconstruction, and after. For the sake of taking in more of the performative

---

49   Paul Laurence Dunbar, "Ere Sleep Comes Down To Soothe the Weary Eyes," *The Collected Poetry of Paul Laurence Dunbar*, ed. Joanne M. Braxton (Charlottesville and London: University Press of Virginia, 1993), 3–4.

aspects of Dunbar's use of dialect (precisely, how it sounds and looks on the page) here is a small excerpt from the poem.

> Dey is times in life when Nature
>   Seems to slip a cog an' go,
> Jes' a-rattlin' down creation,
>   Lak an ocean's overflow;
> When de worl' jes' stahts a-spinnin'
>   Lak a picaninny's top,
> An' yo' cup o' joy is brimmin'
>   'Twell it seems about to slop,
> An' you feel jes' lak a racah,
>   Dat is trainin' fu' to trot—[50]

Dunbar is a figure we should understand first and foremost as troubled by having ambitions for one particular type of poetry (the traditional lyric) but receiving great audience response for another type of poetry (the rural dialect). His tribute poems, such as "Fredrick Douglass," "Douglass," "Robert Gould Shaw," and "The Colored Soldiers," give a sense of the level of the poet's ambition: he sought to have his poetry enter the public register of national memory, as would a great monument or edifice. The success of his dialect poems leaves us with a sense that poems like "We Wear the Mask" and, later, "Sympathy" (in which Dunbar penned the phrase, "I know why the caged bird sings!") speak to the plight of the poet himself. Before long Dunbar discovered himself to be hemmed in by his blackness, and his response—how many options could he have had?—was this formal and tonal discursiveness on the plight of being heard but not being heard that

---

50   Paul Laurence Dunbar, "When De Co'n Pone's Hot," *Collected Poetry*, 57–58.

has left Dunbar as a great mystery to critics and admirers alike. To read Dunbar now is like looking at a bas-relief. His is a drama of background and foreground; and to read one poem in search of Dunbar never suffices, for his crux was, like Lowell's, of a plurality of poems wrought by thirst and dissatisfaction. As I write this I recognize how this should be the case for every poet, that one poem does not capture the poet. But it was never dramatized in African-American poetry with such clarity and poignancy before Paul Laurence Dunbar. And in this sense, despite wading in the waters of the end of the nineteenth century, Dunbar is the originary moment, his crux the archetypal conundrum, of twentieth-century African-American poetry. As W. E. B. Du Bois wrote so famously in 1903, "the problem of the Twentieth Century is the problem of the color-line." And for Dunbar, that line was real and terrible: a suffocating border by which his sense of two poetries sat separate, and forever irreconcilable.

Du Bois, in that same text, *The Souls of Black Folk*, introduced each chapter with a bar of musical notation as a sign of the roots from which African-American writing and thought developed, but also tantalizingly as a trope of the untranslatable and emergent relationship between music and the written word. Since poems create and manage their distinctive cadence through rhythm, meter, punctuation, and the juggling and jarring of consonants and vowels by means of assonance and alliteration, music in this sense has long been regarded as a dynamic internal to a poem. In other words, a poem is made by music and that music consists of words clustering the space on a page. While I am hesitant to turn to particular and inherent differences in an African-American poem from another type of poem, it is nevertheless impossible to ignore the strong and seemingly unshakeable correlation between music and African-American poetry. Music in these instances often emerges as the symptom of, or cure for, a poetic situation. If a lyric poem is generally understood to begin at a moment of disequilibrium in the speaker's sense of the world, and further if poetry can be considered a form of altered speech or altered reckoning, then it is African-American poetry's powerfully successful tendency to revel in music's transformative qualities as a catalyst for poetry that makes for such a unique example of American literary art. Therefore, though there are many varieties of African-American poetry that I could discuss in the space provided, I will instead choose to focus upon music—in particular the blues—and the manner in which music distinguishes itself as a sustentative context by which to understand the evolving impetus behind African-American poetry in the twentieth century.

There are three foundations upon which my understanding of the blues rests: that it began as oral art, that it veers almost compulsively toward repetition, and that it seeks an empathetic though not sympathetic audience—in other words, the blues functions best with a (silently) implicit audience because no matter the problem the blues is not a call for help but rather an itemization of the problem itself. It is a desire embedded within the blues to articulate a problem without servicing it, a crux Ralph Ellison, author of *Invisible Man*, labeled as "tragicomic." While there are poems that expertly emulate the formal aspects of the blues, the *relationship* between the two genres, poetry and music, is best identified in one poem in particular, "The Weary Blues" by Langston Hughes, that circumscribes the blues, literally writing around the blues in order to make a narrative of the effect of the blues upon the speaker, and hence upon the poem itself. The speaker of the poem is situated as a member of the audience enthralled by music so captivating that it becomes the very reason for the poem. But before we approach the blues, let us explore its invisible, and in this case enabling, epigraphic mood.

While there are poems that expertly emulate the formal aspects of the blues, the *relationship* between the two genres, poetry and music, are best identified in one poem in particular that circumscribes the blues, literally writing around the blues in order to make a narrative of the effect of the blues upon the speaker, and hence upon the poem itself. The poem we will be speaking of situates the speaker of the poem as a member of the audience enthralled by music so captivating that it becomes the very reason for the poem. But first an aside . . .

When asked by Countee Cullen to join him at a reading at the 135th Street Branch Library, Hughes balked at the idea of the public spectacle and in his place sent with Cullen a "verse" to be read on Hughes's behalf.

> Ay ya!
> Ay ya!
> Ky ya na mina,
> Ky ya na mina.
> So lee,
> So lee nakyna.
> Ky ya na mina,
> Ky ya na mina.[51]

This uncollected scrap of verse by Hughes, one that mockingly answers the desire for Hughes's presence with indecipherable Africa-

---

51   Arnold Rampersad, *The Life of Langston Hughes: vol. 1, 1902–1941, I, Too, Sing America* (New York: Oxford University Press, 1988), 64.

tinged sound, is to call your attention to the fact that the next poem Hughes would write turned out to be precisely "The Weary Blues." Perhaps the central poem of the Hughes oeuvre, it makes clear for the first time the true extent of the poet's ambition as well as the poet's sense of artistic separation and alienation from the sound and posture of music and the musician. It reminds us now that the contexts by which Black writers came to write novels and stories in the nineteenth century still had deep, perhaps permanent resonance for poets in the twentieth century. Paul Gilroy's remarks regarding "the rise of the novel" in Black nineteenth-century cultural production as yet only in part the "story" of the path to freedom and "the redemptive power of suffering" is, in my view, also a "story" in and of itself. What Gilroy's comments on the nineteenth century foreshadow is the strain of the author in the context of freedom to control "their imaginative humanity" from the power of popular culture to create allegories of their imagined selves.

> The power of the text was qualified and contextualized by the emergence of a more significant counterpower in the medium of black popular culture, what we can call, following Houston A. Baker, Jr., the tactics of sound developed as a form of black metacommunication in a cultural repertoire increasingly dominated by music, dance, and performance.[52]

Consequently, poets of the twentieth century such as Hughes and Phillips have sought to recapture the poetic imagination by seizing back the imaginative focus of an individualized artist by

---

52   Paul Gilroy, *The Black Atlantic: Modernity and Double Consciousness* (Cambridge, Mass.: Harvard University Press, 1993), 201.

contending first with the allegory of that Black artist. For Hughes, this allegorical encounter was something different from Phillips's restless dissent. Hughes instead is an admiring observer, a poet in the role of audience where if we look closely we shall discover the roots of a unique form of poetic frustration.[53]

> Droning a drowsy syncopated tune,
> Rocking back and forth to a mellow croon,
>   I heard a Negro play.
> Down on Lenox Avenue the other night
> By the pale dull pallor of an old gas light
>   He did a lazy sway . . .
>   He did a lazy sway . . .
> To the tune o' those Weary Blues.
> With his ebony hands on each ivory key
> He made that poor piano moan with melody.
>   O Blues!
> Swaying to and fro on his rickety stool
> He played that sad raggy tune like a musical fool.
>   Sweet Blues!
> Coming from a black man's soul.
>   O Blues!
> In a deep song voice with a melancholy tone
> I heard that Negro sing, that old piano moan—
>   "Ain't got nobody in all this world,
>   Ain't got nobody but ma self.
>   I's gwine to quit ma frownin'
>   And put ma troubles on the shelf."

---

53 Although Coleridge's "Kubla Kahn" may in fact be a similar type of poem.

Thump, thump, thump, went his foot on the floor.
He played a few chords then he sang some more—
 "I got the Weary Blues
And I can't be satisfied.
Got the Weary Blues
And can't be satisfied—
I ain't happy no mo'
And I wish that I had died."
And far into the night he crooned that tune.
The stars went out and so did the moon.
The singer stopped playing and went to bed
While the Weary Blues echoed through his head.
He slept like a rock or a man that's dead.[54]

Notice how the poem organizes the experience it describes. Though the poem seeks, at first glance, to say "I saw this, it happened like so," we discover that there is no turn after this occurs in the poem. The typical curve of a poem of this sort—and here I mean those poems that seek to re-imagine significant experience—adds the element of "and therefore I did so" or "and thus I am like so." For example, John Keats gives his reader a sense of what happened to him after first reading Chapman's translation of Homer; and Elizabeth Bishop, after coming face to face with the venerable hook-bearded fish she caught, lets the fish go. Yet "The Weary Blues" stops far short of giving a sense of the altered life or action of the speaker. In fact, "I" only appears twice in order to locate the passive relationship between the speaker of the poem and the blues singer. What, then, is the objective of the start

54 Langston Hughes, "The Weary Blues," *The Collected Poems of Langston Hughes*, ed. Arnold Rampersad (New York: Knopf, 1995), 50.

of the poem where the speaker seems more active ("droning" and "rocking back and forth") though lulled by the context of listening to the music? By starting in such a manner the poem seems to indicate that the poem will discover the transformative effect on the speaker of the poem by being in contact with the blues singer. Yet the active nature of the speaker fades into description, leaving the singer supposedly to his environment. Precisely at the moment in the poem where experience is expected to be condensed into insight or invocation—poems, after all, supposedly delight and instruct—is where one is left with an image of the musician, and only the musician, at a moment of rest; the musician in the rare and sublime moment of not-being-the-musician. Hughes here is deferring pleasure within the poem: a blues-like sacrifice for the sake of an aspiring kinship with the power of a cultural (and racial) icon.

Hughes's poem is a hopeful poem, though not hopeful for a simplistic change in social fortune. Instead the poem is hopeful that it can make art, as the blues singer makes art; the poem aspires to affect the emotions and sensibilities of a person outside of the poem in the way that the blues singer has done to him. Sympathy is not the main emotional register here. The poem behaves as it does in the hopes of establishing an empathy with the blues that it, as of yet, does not possess. Hence the end of the poem should be read as a type of subjunctive mood in which the poet wants to speak of something as though it plainly exists but the parameters of that possibility still chafe with doubt. Simply put: ask yourself, how does the speaker of the poem know of the scene that occurs in the final three lines of the poem?

The singer stopped playing and went to bed
While the Weary Blues echoed through his head.
He slept like a rock or a man that's dead.

Romanticism in particular stretched beautifully for this type of sublimity, this omniscience. But the very process of doing so was also rendered as content in the movement of the poem. Poems like Coleridge's "Frost at Midnight" made explicit the desire for the poetic voice to seize this type of omniscience as the self joins with the world outside of itself. It is an attempt at a poetics, a theory behind the making of the poem. But "The Weary Blues" is a poem that depends on a sense of narrative realism in which the interruption of the events by song is the only phenomenon that subdues a desire within the poem to describe as concisely as possible what it observes.

A cursory approach to reading this poem, as we have been encouraged to read many African-American poems, would ask new readers to regard the manner in which the poem provides a space for the blues singer to speak for himself, in his own words, and to regard the community-building aspects of a poem based, such as this one, on the blues. The Langston Hughes poem "Jazz Band in a Parisian Cabaret" is a poem far more in keeping with this type of thesis than is "The Weary Blues."[55] "Jazz Band" contains a number of speaking characters, emphasized even further by the various languages at play in the poem. The concept is that jazz can bring people together as a common denominator of human interest. The poem's ending—"Can I go home wid yuh, sweetie? / Sure."—is a monosyllabic response to the question, "Can I join

55   Langston Hughes, "Jazz Band in a Parisian Cabaret," *Collected Poems* (New York: Knopf, 1995), 60.

you at your home?" and is spoken by an unidentified character in the poem, but the spacing of the line with the other indented lines leads one to believe that it is more background noise and different from the main speaker in the poem. This is a poem that allows its described participants to, if you will, take the poem over.

"The Weary Blues" defers pleasure in music for the sake of what I earlier referred to as an "aspiring kinship"—but it aspires to the *power* of the icon, not for a kinship *with* the icon itself. The poem does not provide a space for the blues singer's words in order to enliven our sense of the blues singer. The poem, after all, closes with the blues singer being spoken for and described in private by an outside voice. The two characters, we should never forget, are strangers and the candid vision of one offered by the other has not been garnered by familiarity but rather by poetic ambition. The concluding vision is an entreaty for privacy for the sake, at all costs, of poetic vision. One must remember that the blues singer is not provided a space in "The Weary Blues" to speak; he is permitted a stage on which to perform. The dynamic between the speaker of the poem and the blues singer is that of audience to performer, and that does not change. What does change is the power of the speaker of the poem: passive description gives way to the sublimity of what, in the end, may only be temporary omniscience.

I have added "temporary" to "omniscience" here in order to emphasize the subdued sense of hope and threat in the poem. Again, the most readily available reading of the poem is that it seeks to give a voice and stage to those who have generally been outsiders to the topics and themes of American poetry. This is one of the great interventions of the poetry of the Harlem Renaissance: it provided portraits of (urban) African-American popular art. Yet as we have seen, the voice of the blues singer is only the voice of performance (are people the same on stage as they are off?), and consequently, the conclusion of the poem is deceptively a homage to the ability of poetic vision to see beyond its given locale (a locale clearly put forth as setting in line four of the poem, "Down on Lenox Avenue"). In this sense, "The Weary Blues" is a type of experiment in poetry in which the poet seeks to incorporate the thus far untamed and mystified subject of the blues. Hughes is approaching the blues in a moment before genre; there is no body of work in 1923 known as the blues poem to the extent that, in 1973, there so clearly was. He is, to dig up a phrase, in the wilds of literary history. Consequently, the task here for the poet is to make the wild, or Dionysian, coalesce with the calm and meditative—what would be traditional poetics—or the Apollonian.

Hughes starts the poem with a rhymed couplet in iambic pentameter, reminiscent of the heroic couplet most strongly identified with Alexander Pope and John Dryden. But the third line severs the traditionalism of that initial couplet: "I heard a Negro play." It is the introduction of the performer and of the blues that makes the poem veer from its original structure. We should also compare the poeticized diction of the couplet—"Droning," "drowning," "syncopated tune," "back and forth," "mellow croon"—with the plain succinctness of the intruding third line: "I heard a Negro play." From that moment on, until the final five lines of the poem, "The Weary Blues" is an intertexture of two types of poetry and the objective is to find a poetics by which both can function as one. This is a supremely ambitious poem whose task is to answer poetic ambition, not to give voice to another. The voice seeks to incorporate the voice of another within its own. The hope is that the would-be *ars poetica* succeeds; the threat, felt as it is in the process of becoming, is that it may not. But this is where lyric poems find their balance and emotive power. Hughes is here working through a poem with an immense bravery behind a poetics that strays from the easy path of sentimentality for its perceived subject, the blues singer, to the fraught and tenacious possibility that the poet and the poet's ambition here are the subject. The last five lines of the poem are a taste of poetic inspiration (from the Latin "breathe into") in which the poet has, in the end, literally breathed into the blues and swallowed whole the perceived subject into the body of a poem, scored by ambition and brought forth by a music external to its first two intertwined metrical lines. The word "weary" in "The Weary Blues" is as much about the effort of the poet to incorporate what is not the poet's as it is about the worldly fatigue of the maestro of the blues.

Hughes's problem here with the blues is an archetypal circumstance for the poet in regard to music. He finds that he cannot at this point consolidate without interruption the formal properties of the blues with those more traditionally aligned with the poet. To transcribe inherently oral material, which is what Hughes is doing with the sung parts of the poem, is likewise a momentary turn of the poet into stenographer. Structurally, this problem is dramatized by the use of couplets—rhymed and, in the beginning, metrical, these couplets are rather self-consciously made—to emphasize the distinction between the two patterns. This is why, though the poet has the last word in the poem, the poem ends when the blues singer stops playing and leaves. The poet is modeling a problem of poetic influence in formal terms. As Hughes portrays the singer in a deep sleep, it is the singer's soundlessness, and thus the poet's inability to continue the poem, that in the end brings up the possibility of the singer's destruction. For in the end, the poet has little access to the private life of the singer save by way of the blues singer's enthralling performance and the poet's inspired momentary poetic vision. The end of the performance reveals a need on the part of the poet, which is represented as a private horror, an anxiety over the end of poetry itself. Music transcends language and can transcend place and identity. We believe that we appreciate and even "understand" music despite either the absence of lyrics or of lyrics we can understand. Can poetry hold up to such a standard? For African-American poetry, which was to become more and more intertwined with African-American music as the twentieth century progressed, the presence of music was to become the great challenging question: if music can reach and affect so many and produce what Wordsworth called in his definition of the lyric poem "a spontaneous overflow of powerful emotions," then what would be the role of poetry? Is poetry in the process of being replaced? And, in this vein, is "The Weary Blues" a response?

"The Weary Blues" is a staggering example of the effect that music can have on the design of a poem. While many poems have been, in terms of their content, about music, no poems before "The Weary Blues" dramatized the context under which African-American poetry and African-American music fought for the same stage. Hughes's poem is a coded poetics: a tale of poetic antagonism that does not rob the reader or steal from the critic its surface impression of being a tribute to the blues and blues performers. And yet, like all poems that withstand our considerable attention and probing, "The Weary Blues" embeds a story within a story. Poets, especially, are often intrigued by the story within the story in a poem: the narrative of what the poem intends by changing from one type of stanza to another, from one voice to another, how a poem ends where it began. Thus the manner by which poets after "The Weary Blues" have sought to address or circumvent the circumstances and "problems" contextualized by African-American music and poetry are various and telling.

Hughes's contemporary, and one of the most underappreciated poets of the past century, Sterling A. Brown, used humor in some instances to play with the assumption that African-Americans have a more innate relationship to the blues. In his poem "Slim Greer" the protagonist, Slim, is a playful character who constantly finds his way in and out of trouble. Slim is in Arkansas and is passing for white. Passing is a situation in which people of color who do not appear to possess features common to the stereotypical conception of a racial type either do not reveal their racial identity or state explicitly that they are of another racial designation in order to avoid the hardships of segregation and discrimination. Though Slim is a very dark man he is able, strangely, to pass. Brown is writing here in the tragicomic mode common both to the blues and its distant cousin, the ballad.

> How he in Arkansas
> Passed for white,
> An' he no lighter
> Than a dark midnight.

> Found a nice white woman
> At a dance,
> Thought he was from Spain
> Or else from France

Only one person has a doubt regarding Slim's racial identity, and that person—despite Slim's "midnight dark" complexion—is suspicious rather than certain. One subsequent day the suspicious "Hill Billy," a character in the poem who was also competing for the affection of the aforementioned woman, pays this same woman a visit and finds Slim there already and "comfy." It is when Slim decides to play the piano that all of the Hill Billy's suspicions end:

> Heard Slim's music—
> An' then, hot damn!
> Shouted sharp—"Nigger!"
> An' Slim said, "Ma'am?"[56]

Music in this instance speaks more to the way in which others have chosen to identify African-Americans than to how music plays a part in the life of Slim Greer. In this context one may see the way in which music can define an individual (in this case racially) rather than the individual choosing to be defined.

"Slim Greer" is a ballad and accordingly observes the tendency of ballads to create a heroic and/or tragic figure. Music in African-American poetry has also been the template upon which heroism, at times a tragic heroism, makes its mark. For example, Robert Hayden's "Homage to the Empress of the Blues" strikes a subtle note for the situations under which performers and musicians share their love for musical expression. The structure of the poem is cause and effect—because this happened, this happened—and it is deployed stanzaically, the first and third stanzas serving as causes and the second and fourth the effects. What is striking about the poem is that the causes are not clearly correlative

---

56   Sterling A. Brown, "Slim Greer," *The Collected Poems of Sterling A. Brown*, ed. Michael S. Harper (Evanston: TriQuarterly, 1989), 77–78.

to the resultant fact—that Bessie Smith, famed "Empress of the Blues," sang. Yet the poem alludes to the sense that the dangers explicit in the first and third stanzas are implicit in the power of the performance of Bessie Smith. Their suffering, spelled out in the first stanza, is answered by the beauty and elegance of the singing woman; their apprehension, identified in the third stanza, of leaving their safe-though-not-so-safe interior world of a blues tavern, is pardoned by the beauty and elegance of the singing woman. The poem does not center on a transformative power of Bessie Smith and her blues; rather, "Homage to the Empress of the Blues" takes the perspective of the enraptured member of the audience, who takes Bessie Smith's relevance as an emergent act of artistry amidst and arisen from within hard life. Consequently, Hayden here provides a definition of the blues through this poem. The blues manages somehow to make a collective out of individual suffering, and through the formation of this collective finds resolution by means of coping as opposed to resolving. The blues does not suggest cures; the blues is its own cure.

The manner by which the blues seeks to inspire a resiliency of the individual finds root often in repetition. Langston Hughes used what is typically referred to as a blues stanza for the voice of the blues singer. This stanza has in it a repetitive engine.

> I got the Weary Blues
> And I can't be satisfied.
> Got the Weary Blues
> And can't be satisfied—
> I ain't happy no mo'
> And I wish that I had died.

The idea behind repetition is that it is a mnemonic device: it aids in remembering something. Why would someone want to remember that they have the blues? Because the blues is an anodyne for a troubled soul. In "Deep Song" by Gayl Jones, we find a poem that forgoes the blues stanza and focuses on repetition. By doing so the poem is imbued with a sense of resilience weighted down by weariness.

> The blues calling my name.
> She is singing a deep song.
> She is singing a deep song.
> and further along in the poem
> I care about you.
> I care.
> I care about you.
> I care.[57]

This is an example of a formal aspect of African-American music, the resonance of repetition in the blues, being reproduced by a poem. The compulsion to repeat, both in this poem and generally in the blues, leads to clear (though not unproblematic) statement. Therefore, the repetition observed is actually incremental: a building up of material for effect. If the effect here is to say, "I love you," the poem acts as a dramatization of what one goes through regardless of (or despite) saying those three words. The general simplicity of the poem and muted epiphany of its end provide a mysterious quality that is technical as much as it is situational. Repetition here implies contemplation, which is the structural dynamic by which the blues is

---

57   Gayl Jones, "Deep Song," *The Iowa Review* 6:2 (Spring, 1975): 11.

an attempt to work through problematic situations—though it should be noted that because its poetic effect is more linear than stanzaic, the poem echoes the structures of jazz more than it does the blues.

Behind the Music

I have attempted to present a few of what I consider to be the more provocative contexts within which African-American poets have contextualized the blues and jazz. There are many more contexts and even more poets who have recreated or responded to the great challenge that music is for the writer. The poems created from these contexts have touched, for instance, the formal precision of the ancient Japanese form of the haiku. Etheridge Knight asserts with the last haiku of his poem entitled "Haiku" that

> Making jazz swing in
> seventeen syllables AIN'T
> no square poet's job.[58]

And the experimentalist nature of Nathaniel Mackey's poetics has given us poems rich in musical dreamscapes that in their arabesque syntax occupy a space somewhere between refinement and tantrum. With Jimi Hendrix in mind, Mackey's "Black Snake Visitation" repeats lines that invoke both the dedication to practice and the torque of madness that both poet and musician typically occupy:

---

58   Etheridge Knight, "Haiku," *The Essential Etheridge Knight* (Pittsburgh: University of Pittsburgh Press, 1986), 17–18.

been rehearsing,
lizardquick
tongues like

they were licking
the sky.[59]

There is a sense in Yusef Komunyakaa's poetry of the modern urban man increasingly isolated from his surroundings and from himself, spared only somewhat by music present or by the memory of music. In his "Untitled Blues" the poem turns quickly, unexpectedly, from observing a photo of a poor black boy to a subjunctive-laden invocation of the calming effects of music.

Sure, I could say everything's copacetic,
listen to a Buddy Bolden cornet
cry from one of those coffin-
shaped houses called
shotgun.[60]

Music here does not interrupt a stream of thought to provide clarity or poignancy. Instead music here is an option weighed and discarded by the speaker. Thus, not only does Komunyakaa present the speaker of the poem as being a devotee of music, but he also presents us with an aspect of authorial control that serves as the poem's antecedent scenario. In other words, the speaker of the poem is so comfortable with music that he can offer a tune as

59   Nathaniel Mackey, "Black Snake Visitation," *Eroding Witness* (Urbana and Chicago: University of Illinois Press, 1985), 19–21.
60   Yusef Komunyakaa, "Untitled Blues," *Neon Vernacular: New and Selected Poems* (Hanover and London: Wesleyan University Press, 1993), 64.

the immediate response to poignant memory and then dismiss it. This is a small and yet significant reimagining of the role of jazz and blues in the work of poets.

Finally, I would like to briefly discuss Michael S. Harper's use of the dramatic monologue as it pertains to jazz and blues performers of the past. If "The Weary Blues" produces a poetic amanuensis for the experiences of the blues singer, the dramatic monologues of Michael S. Harper are the responsive opposite. They provide a context and situations by which blues and jazz performers reveal an inner life and complex psychologies either before or in the midst of creating their music.

While poetry previously attempted to celebrate these musicians by means of encomium or replication, Harper's dramatic monologues delve into the antecedent scenarios of music's creation by giving a depth and interiority to musicians. Poems like "A Narrative of the Life and Times of John Coltrane: Played by Himself" answer the poetic problem outlined in "The Weary Blues" by turning the situation of poetry inside-out: the musician is now the poet, and the poet—the one writing, or "playing" the poem—is the musician. The first stanza reveals some of the pain that Coltrane suffered from during performance. Consider the difference between a poem stating that from a third person perspective and how the effect works here as a dramatic narrative. The poem goes on to provide aspects of Coltrane's life *between* shows; a look into the Coltrane the audience is distanced from. The end of the poem reveals Coltrane's sense of weariness but admixes that as well with an expressive desire to break from addiction—but not just an addiction to heroin; an addiction, as well, to routine:

And then, on a train to Philly,
I sang "Naima" locking the door
without exit no matter what song
I sang; with remonstrations on the ceiling
of that same room I practiced in
on my back when too tired to stand,
I broke loose from crystalline habits
I thought would bring me that sound.[61]

Harper's poems prove to be an original turn in subject and tone. They also seduce with an instructive gravity. The poem is not subordinate to biography, instead these types of poems radiate in their ability to do what neither a reproduction of the music or a biography could do: they make aspects of the life repeatable, if only momentarily. The reader becomes John Coltrane. The poem is the thought made by the reader, as Coltrane, as the poem is read. One thus approaches an empathetic sensibility instead of a sympathetic one. And thus, the twentieth century seems farther and farther away from the theme of sentimentality with which the nineteenth century closed. Rich dramatic monologues like "A Narrative on the Life and Times of John Coltrane: Played by Himself" are also the poetic successors of "The Weary Blues"—and as such we should be thankful for that peculiar habit poets have of speaking *as* someone else instead of *for* someone else.

---

61   Michael S. Harper, "A Narrative of the Life and Times of John Coltrane: Played By Himself," *Songlines in Michaeltree: New and Collected Poems* (Urbana and Chicago: University of Illinois Press), 187–188.

DEREK WALCOTT:

IMAGINATION, NATION, AND THE POETICS OF MEMORY

Along the sandy reach of Fort James, Antigua, the shoreline still supports the sparse colonial keepsake cannons, but a few patches of mottled tarmac remain of what once was a road. Hurricane Luis, a massive category-four event, struck in early September 1995 and leveled the islands of Antigua and Barbuda. Like an indifferent colossus made of harbor and sea it brought back its bow of storm and struck; the damage to the island was cataclysmic. Where the hungry surf swallows the road is a reminder; and the once full and familiar shape of the beach is now thinner, more sallow. Indeed—though still beautiful—there is simply less of it. Over by Dickinson Bay, a similar coastal duress still shows its wounds. The case is similar for nearly all of Antigua's beaches and stony shoals. For Antigua is shrinking, bit by bit.

Each hurricane brings with it howling storms and clawing waves that paw the sand further and further away from the shore, dragging fragments of Antigua into the Caribbean Sea that curls below it and the Atlantic Ocean that expands above it. If you return to Antigua intermittently you are always liable to find a different island than the one you last saw. The islandness of it may seem the same, but the sea has taken back much of Antigua. Surrounded by the sunshine reflecting off the shimmering still-life of the sea are bits of the island that dissipate with each tug of the salt-soaked surf. What will the citizens of Antigua, which gained independence in 1981, think of the shape of their new but shrinking nation in 2081?

Larger islands like Puerto Rico may not share this admittedly apocalyptic concern of mine. Yet certainly the issue of nation is a pertinent, perhaps axiomatic, concern to that place. It also has its apt and quiet metaphors. In Aguadilla, a medium-sized town on the northwest coast of the island, there is half a graveyard tee-tering on the edge of the sea like a loose tooth. Another spite-ful storm sucked in a number of graves and headstones, leaving cenotaphs in their place. Aguadilla is the birthplace of poet and statesman José de Diego. Some of his verses rest in that graveyard slope in the sun toward the ocean, though the poet himself was buried among the distingué in Old San Juan. A staunch activist for Puerto Rican independence until his death in 1918, de Diego founded the Academia Antillas de la Lengua (Antillean Academy of Language) in defense of the Spanish language in 1915. He was referred to among his admirers by the sobriquet "el Caballero de la Raza" (loosely, "knight of the race"). Diego's most well-known poem is probably the elegiac "A Laura," a love poem that has since remained within the memory of various Puerto Rican communi-ties and is a well-wrought fragment of national consciousness. The Laura in question, a lost love still alive when de Diego wrote the poem while studying in Barcelona, eventually went mad and took to reciting the poem as she wandered. After her death, de Diego wrote "Póstuma," a few stanzas of which emblazon a sepulcher high up in the storm-raked graveyard, having survived what must at times seem the cannibalistic temperament of the sea.

Landmasses small and smaller in the Caribbean weather the changes of larger nations. The poets from this region often at one point or another find themselves either attempting to herald a tradition or jack-knifing a foreign one. Nations have been granted the right to call themselves such with a limp tongue or have been encouraged to dismiss the entire enterprise altogether as a pitiable carrot for the passé. What is a nation? That should be a simple question to pose to a chain of islands separated not only by water but often by language as well. Simple?

The Caribbean has always been a subject of speculative vision as a mode of Western desire. From the travel narratives and maps of explorers and cartographers to the glossy mass media of tourist agencies and tourist boards, what the Caribbean gives of itself to the "First World" has been largely a matter of eye candy.[62] Even in its aural evocations—zouke, reggae, salsa, calypso, and such—the arts of the Caribbean have been overburdened by a glut of exportable visual signs for foreign consumers. Always the apt pupil, the Caribbean has become quite skilled at repeating

---

62   Some provocative analyses of the interplay of colonialism, slavery, and visual representation include Michael Palencia-Roth, "Mapping the Caribbean: Cartography and the Cannibalization of Culture," in *A History of Literature of the Caribbean, Volume 3: Cross-Cultural Studies,* ed. A. James Arnold (Amsterdam: John Benjamins, 1994), 3–27; Robert J.C. Young, *Colonial Desire: Hybridity in Theory, Culture, and Race* (London: Routledge, 1995); and Marcus Wood's *Blind Memory: Visual Representations of Slavery in England and America, 1780–1863* (London: Routledge, 2000).

those signs of itself as itself. But the politics of these types of visual metanarratives hardly stop with aesthetics. They are, of course, a vital part of the economic and political life of the Caribbean. How does this then relate to its artists?

Before becoming a poet and subsequently one of the great novelists of his generation, Wilson Harris was a geological surveyor for the government of his native Guyana. His extensive knowledge of the Guyanese landscape—its savannahs, rivers, white sand belt, interior highland and rivers—has led to the enrichment of his novels by its prominence as its own distinctive near-character with a pervasive and iconic quality to it. "Instead of acting on a passive landscape with an inquisitive, romantic or even scientific imagination," writes the poet Fred D'Aguiar, "Harris found that his experience as a surveyor in Guyana's Amazonian interior changed *how* he imagined. Landscape informed his utterance and defined the very makeup of the expression of the story."[63] Twenty-three novels later, to look back now at the poetry of Wilson Harris what stands out most is the dramatic change in his vision of landscape. Classical, primordial and above all allegorical, Harris's poems transfigured Guyana into a world of public and private significations (which, in retrospect, makes a world of sense for an ambitious young writer employed by the government to survey the land). "I found it impossible to write what I felt, but persisted. There were clues in ancient Homer speaking of the gods as animals and birds arising and descending from spaces in and above the earth. This reminded me of the pre-Columbian god Quetzalcoatl, *quetzal* (the bird), *coatl* (the snake). There were clues in the one-eyed Cyclops that I now saw standing like

---

63   Fred D'Aguiar, "Wilson Harris," *Bomb* 82 (Winter, 2002/2003): 76.

a lightning-struck tree in the forest. But such clues came home to me as 'museum pieces' divorced from their genuine and original sources. I had never felt such a divorce so acutely, so sharply before. I had accepted it all along as natural." Harris continues, "My busy activities were all that action was. Now, however, in the depths of the multiform pressures of what seemed other than the nature I had known, in the sudden station of a tree, in the sudden station of a rock, like watchers that were potently alive, potently still, there was *something else*, something akin to a bloodstream of spirit that ran everywhere with an astonishing momentum that made my former activities pale into a fixity or immobility."[64] The result was *Eternity to Season*, a collection of poems constantly poised between the living world and the pre-life/afterlife, the material world and the immaterial world. The epigraph to the book is "Every living being is also a fossil" and should be considered against his lines in the poem "The Well" that "Each step / has its witness and leaves / its record: / turns stone into echoing flesh." The chiasmus of flesh, fossil: stone, flesh marks the Guyanese landscape as the site within which human change happens, but the repeated sense of the gods talking through nature and the past's speaking insistently through the present gave the work the sense that the imagination was standing before nature and making itself a priority among a natural history of ruin and hope.

Within this context, consider the following reflection by Wilson Harris on national boundaries and artists.

> A friend of mine recently told me that in conversation with a certain high-ranking Guyanese official and politi-

---

64   Ibid.

cian, he discovered that that politician saw landscape as nothing more than the boundaries of his constituency. The ideal artist or scientist for him, therefore, was someone who conformed to an immediate governing stasis of place and time.[65]

The implication being that the difference between artists and the politician's ideal of the artist involves, in part, the way in which the national environment is considered and subsequently rendered. A "governing stasis of place and time" by which only newspapers state the date and maps mark the bureaucrat's zone of indifference houses artists who mimic the newspaper's drone, the bureaucrat's canton. This is beyond the Caribbean in stasis; this is the Caribbean in traction. Fanon writes:

> A world divided into compartments, a motionless, Manicheistic world, a world of statues: the statue of the general who carried out the conquest, the statue of the engineer who built the bridge; a world which is sure of itself, which crushes with its stones the backs flayed by whips: this is the colonial world. The native is being hemmed in; apartheid is simply one form of the division into compartments of the colonial world. The first thing which the native learns is to stay in his place, and not to go beyond certain limits.[66]

---

65   Wilson Harris, "The Amerindian Legacy," *Selected Essays of Wilson Harris: The Unfinished Genesis of the Imagination* (New York: Routledge, 1999), 174.
66   Frantz Fanon, *The Wretched of the Earth*, trans. Constance Farrington (New York: Grove Press, 1963), 51–52.

The opposite of the politician's ideal poet, we should infer, would be prophetic, difficult, a contrarian.

Landscape, with Nation in It

Hence, I find myself thinking of poets and their always (hopefully) problematic relationship to nations. Poets in particular, if not bathed in dogma (though no one can claim freedom from some ideological underpinning), face the harrowing task of creating representations of the world with tools that, like the shores, are always swallowing themselves: poets use words. And despite the fact that poetry is the great card trick of making houses with aces and spades, people continue to live under the poet's unstable tools. To exist linguistically is to be in a relationship with a poet, some poet. Whether lyric, epic or dramatic, verse calls attention to one voice's way of saying the world and necessarily acts as a counterpoint to other uses of the same language. Either it is a hopeful mimetic of a way of representing a language or it startles against the conventions of common usage.

Both poetry and nation link etymologically to creation. "Poetry," coming from the Greek *poiesis*, or "making," also implies a relationship to home and to the body in its uses of the Italian word for "room," *stanza*; its invocation of "foot" as the term for the basic metric unit of verse; and dactyl (Latin for "finger") for a particular foot that, like any finger on your left hand, has one long unit and two shorter ones. "Nation," meanwhile, echoes the Latin *nasci*, "to be born," and its obvious equivalents in modern languages are the Spanish verb *nacer*, as well as the French *naître*. Thus, in any examination of the relationship between poetry and the idea of nation, one also is witness to a parthenogenetic event: a simultaneous situation of making and of being born.

Shabine, protagonist of the poem "The Schooner *Flight*," was one such character. A sailor and poet who spent most of his life at sea, within the schooner *Flight* as within "The Schooner *Flight*" he reflects on how geography has formed his fate.

> I know these islands from Monos to Nassau,
> a rusty head sailor with sea-green eyes
> that they nickname Shabine, the patois for
> any red nigger, and I, Shabine, saw
> when these slums of empire was paradise.
> I'm just a red nigger who love the sea,
> I had a sound colonial education,
> I have Dutch, nigger, and English in me,
> and either I'm nobody, or I'm a nation.[67]

This passage, early in the long poem, concludes on the idea of nation, yet one should note as well how heavily invested the lines are in both the strategy of naming and the strategy of self-definition. Though Shabine first asserts that he knows the vast stretches of the archipelago, he undercuts this assertion with a simple and quick admission of how he received his name. "Shabine" is not only patois, itself a differentiated mode of speaking from an imperial language, but what it signifies ("just a red nigger") is an accentuation of that linguistic difference as a reductive and metonymic agent. Yet, as poetry is concentrated language, we find that in this brief

---

67 Derek Walcott, "The Schooner *Flight*," *Collected Poems 1948–1984* (New York: Farrar, Straus and Giroux, 1986), 346.

passage Shabine re-inscribes almost every assignation that originally circumscribed him. The "I" is situated first, as speech comes before recognition. Then the metaphoric recognition of the self in other objects, in this case an admixture of a nail with the sea: "a rusty head sailor with sea-green eyes." A pronoun enters the passage to provide a name. This is where the passage turns. Let's look at the role that the texture of Walcott's lines play in this.

> I know these islands from Monos to Nassau,
> a rusty head sailor with sea-green eyes

The first line is a statement of knowledge in which the predicate ("these islands from Monos to Nassau") states a claim (I know all of the Caribbean) while demonstrating it ("these islands from Monos to Nassau">"all of the Caribbean">"this region from end to end"). Knowledge in this sense reveals itself as experience. It also subtly makes the statement of knowledge both autobiographical (I have been to these places) and an unstable signifier (i.e., if you neither know where Monos nor Nassau are you may or may not get the point of what Shabine is saying) that therefore leaves only one recipient of the knowledge claim undeniably accounted for: Shabine himself. The second line is a moment of self-perception separate, as Plato argued, from knowledge itself. Shabine is able to perceive himself based on objects that undoubtedly were around him: nails that held his boat together and that grew rust from their contact with the sea; that same sea sharing the green hue of his eyes. We can know without perceiving and we can perceive without knowing. Thus, Shabine's knowledge of his region, of his geography is a thing apart from how he sees himself. That the poet maintains the grammatical integrity of the lines reinforces this. That the lines lose this integrity to enjambment and the intrusion of "they" reinforces this further.

> that they nickname Shabine, the patois for
> any red nigger

With the introduction/intrusion of others, of "they," we are introduced to "Shabine," a false name we learn was given to him (before he was "I"). "Shabine" brings with it a split in the rhythmic unit: the break caused by the caesura after the name; the enjambment; weak-ending with the prepositional "for" and then the subsequent cleft of the pentameter with "any red nigger." The passage has moved from subject-centered knowledge (I know") to object-transferred dismissiveness ("any red nigger"). And what follows encourages its reader to regard the half-line as also a split in the semantic unit:

> and I Shabine, saw
> when these slums of empire was paradise.

The resultant effect is rife with paradox. While forming a portrait of the artist (lest we forget that while a seaman, Shabine also is a poet), the passage pits Shabine's ontological naming against his own articulation of his self, and culminates that filtered articulation with the evocation of the self as a perceiving, metaphorizing subject. Though named through metaphor and racial assignation, the poem, like a fulcrum, teeters upon the beats of the "and I," where the change from object to subject is again realized in its reconsideration of his birth as the poet and protagonist "Shabine."

That this crucial line ends with "saw" and enjambs Shabine's historical-romantic vision highlights the interdependence of these lines as a unit through which to understand how Shabine's ability to interpret is strongly wedded to how he has been interpreted. Walcott foreshadows this interplay of name and self-realization in his earlier poem "Names."

Names

My race began as the sea began,
with no horizon,
with pebbles under my tongue,
with a different fix on the stars.
But now my race is here,
in the sad oil of Levantine eyes,
in the flags of Indian fields.
I began with no memory,
I began with no future,
but I looked for that moment
when the mind was halved by the horizon.
I have never found that moment
when the mind was halved by the horizon—
for the goldsmith from Benares,
the stonecutter from Canton,
as a fishline sinks, the horizon
sinks in the memory.
Have we melted into a mirror,
leaving our souls behind?
The goldsmith from Benares,
the stonecutter from Canton,

the bronzesmith from Benin.

A sea-eagle screams from the rock,

and my race began like the osprey

with that cry,

that terrible vowel,

that I!

Behind us all the sky folded

as history folds over a fishline,

and the foam foreclosed

with nothing in our hands

but this stick

to trace our names on the sand

which the sea erased again, to our indifference.[68]

Shabine is, by name and identity, what is around him, and he muses likewise on what surrounds him. His power of rhetoric, however, is spurred beyond the immediacy of his vision. Hence, the proximity of "these slums" becomes distanced by the vague and diffusing nouns of "empire" and "paradise." Shabine's lyrical reconsideration of his birth as "Shabine," from knowledgeable surveyor ("I know these islands from Monos to Nassau") to the clause-cragged invocation of his own name, leads to a more minute and specific rendering of his place. He extends this action, of course, through metaphor. Shabine makes his name a linguistic birth, and we are to assume that the islands, the sea, and the wet and rusted nails that would hold his boat together are the synecdochical parts of this Caribbean individual. From here, the "I, Shabine"—fully and rhetorically intact—makes poetry out of

68   Walcott, "Names," *Collected Poems*, 305–306.

a simple statement of himself similar to a Caribbean Walt Whitman, even down to the anaphora.

> I'm just a red nigger who love the sea,
> I had a sound colonial education,
> I have Dutch, nigger, and English in me,
> and either I'm nobody, or I'm a nation.

In *Poétique de la Relation*, Éduoard Glissant describes a "poetics of language-in-itself [that] sanctions the moment when language, as if satisfied with its perfection, ceases to take for its object the recounting of its connection with particular surroundings, to concentrate solely upon its fervor to exceed its limits and reveal thoroughly the elements composing it—solely upon its engineering skill with these."[69] In a similar vein, we can see that Shabine is actually repeating himself. There is little difference in content between the previous five lines we have been discussing and these succeeding four lines. In fact, the persistent articulation of the "I" in all nine lines should clue a reader in to the delving and desirous theme of self-articulation throughout the passage. Yet, as Glissant suggests, Shabine's language provides extra text almost as if *out of pleasure*, or at least from some sort of satisfaction from the previous summation. The "just" is heavily sarcastic, and the confidence of calling himself "a red nigger" in a full line of iambic pentameter provides a marked difference from the stalled line of "any red nigger, and I, Shabine, saw." Shabine's memory of his name as the object "recounting . . . its connection with its

---

69   Éduoard Glissant, *Poétique de la Relation*, trans. Betsy Wing (Ann Arbor: University of Michigan Press, 1997), 25.

particular surroundings" precedes fallen "paradise" as that which can bypass its "limits" through an evocation of the elements of composition: those things that make up the speaker and that the speaker in turn seeks to make a priori. Walcott has always been an Adamic thinker. Hence, though Shabine basically repeats a composite sketch of himself in these nine lines, the final four serve as a "national romance," but of the self—one that shares no sense of sacrifice toward a utopic space.[70] To understand Shabine correctly, one must remember that he is an individual singled not only by his burning thirst to "say" himself (he certainly seems already to know himself) but also by his desire for domestic and poetic harbor. It is on these terms—Adamic, and almost entirely self-serving—that the poet can claim such a distinction between nobody and nation. Nationalism along these lines, as opposed to those of patriotism, is hardly a loyalty to a body politic. On the contrary, it is a loyalty to the self and the self's potential realizations of itself; for the self supposedly desires—in tandem with the nation—to be (or to become) someone after all. But if "someone" is part of the phenomenon of someone else's consciousness (the context in which "I" and "Shabine" co-exist), what is the effect then, if any, on the reality of the poet.

The Shield of the Caribbean
"I had no nation now but the imagination" begins the third part of "The Schooner *Flight*" and is titled "Shabine Leaves the Republic." The line is much more of a pun than a declaration, more

---

70   For more on "national romance," see Doris Sommer, *Foundational Fictions: The National Romances of Latin America* (Berkeley: University of California Press, 1991).

a mise-en-scene than a statement about the self. Structurally, the line comes immediately after the series of rhetorical questions directed to Christ. And these questions come on the heels of Shabine's failed attempt at sexual satisfaction with other women on the heels of two prior failed romances; one with Maria Concepcion (a failed source of erotic capture), the other with his wife (a failed source of domestic security).

> When I left the madhouse I tried other women
> but, once they stripped naked, their spiky cunts
> bristled like sea-eggs and I couldn't dive.
> The chaplain came round. I paid him no mind.
> Where is my rest place, Jesus? Where is my harbour?
> Where is the pillow I will not have to pay for,
> and the window I can look from that frames my life?[71]

Why is it that immediately following a failed attempt at both sexual and spiritual union that "The Schooner *Flight*" picks up speed again with this quip of nation, identity and the imagination—undoubtedly the most well-known line of the poem? As stated above, the line should be read perhaps more as a pun than as an edict, as Shabine has proven to rely almost entirely upon the instability of language to codify and support his fractured sense of self. Shabine is, in one sense, a character from romance, as his lack of sexual and domestic union has left him now for some reason to declare that he has no nation. This moment is generally read as, first, a matter of Shabine's (read: Walcott's) multi-racial identity leaving him an alien in his own home country. Evidence

---

71 Walcott, "The Schooner *Flight*," 350.

for this observation would seem to be reside in these early lines from "Shabine Leaves the Republic."

> After the white man, the niggers didn't want me
> when the power swing to their side.
> The first chain my hands and apologize, "History";
> the next said I wasn't black enough for their pride.

Yet, Walcott has already written this but little over one hundred lines ago in the "I, Shabine" passage which we discussed. The passage "either I'm nobody or a nation" chases the subject of races down quite succinctly it would seem; and, as stated earlier, it even provides a form of poetic architecture through which Shabine may iterate a new beginning through verse as well as through the idea of nation. "I had no nation now but the imagination" asks a reader to stall and unpack the phrase—the eye rhyme, the internal rhyme, and the alliterative "n's"—and, therefore, as an impediment to reading, leaves a reader still to contend mnemonically with the action antecedent to this passage.

That said, I do not wish to undermine the importance of the sense of racial difference and alienation as a part of Shabine's conception of his relation to nation. Rather, I suggest we draw our attention more to his relationship to Concepcion, which is clearly as vital to his sense of alienation, at least at this moment of the poem, as is his race. "Concepcion" is, of course, Spanish for the act of conception and forms a play on words in and of itself. Walcott, in Maria Concepcion, has created an allegory of religious, conjugal, and creative desire. Doris Sommer's work on the "foundational fictions" of Latin America, those nineteenth-century canonical romantic novels, found that those "sentimental epics" determine for their readership the "erotic and national projects" through allegorical portraiture.[72] They are fictions that "look relentlessly forward [and] set desire into a spiral or zigzagging motion inside a double structure that keeps projecting the narrative into the future as eroticism and patriotism pull each other along."[73] Pun and allegory serve here as that double structure of which Sommer is concerned. And while we should read the split of Shabine's desire between Maria Concepcion and his wife as its own double structure of erotic and domestic desire, we should also note that within the poem neither flaw is mediated in a way that would "overcome the obstacle and [then] consolidate the nation." Sommer concludes that these foundational fictions influence traditional allegory in the sense that they produce a resolution dialectically. That resolution takes the form of "the promise of consolidation," as it "constitutes another level of desire and underscores the erotic goal, which is also a microcosmic expression of nationhood."[74] The connections between Shabine's desirous and increasingly alienated subjectivity and the foundational fictions of Latin America are intriguing. The obvious divergence comes in that Shabine has no institutionalized or locally sanctioned fictions by which to consolidate the nation that does not include his own subjugation. He owns no land ("but for the sea," I am sure he would say), has no title, seems desperately useless anywhere save in a boat or before a page, and apparently loves but two things: poetry and landscape.

72 Sommer, *Foundational Fictions*, 49.
73 Ibid., 46–47.
74 Ibid., 49.

To claim that "I had no nation now but the imagination" is to first of all locate the statement in a particular narrative context: "I had no nation now." Shabine is in the midst of recollection while agitating toward a poetic form. To recollect in poetic form is to attempt to negotiate recollection and repetition. Freud theorizes that recollection is a function of voluntary memory, and repetition is a function of involuntary memory. Instead of debating Freud's theories, I wish to emphasize how a poetics of memory attempts to mediate recollection precisely through repetition instead of at its expense. Poetry repeats by its very nature; syllables and sounds bear the stain of repetition. Only the most sarcastically truncated and self-conscious poem can hope to avoid repetition of any sort. Thus, I read "I had no nation now but the imagination" as Walcott expressing a past situation in that present of the poem's narrative. It is a recollection of a past trauma—that fractured, alienated consciousness recognizing its fracture—but also a repetition of a complaint—the complaint of being nobody's national.

The "now" is a strong beat after the falling "-tion" of "nation" and serves as a narrative link to the just concluded episode of questioning and failure. It hinges the spiritual, erotic, domestic failure of the previous canto to this consideration of a national and political self. The stress upon "now" also introduces another caesura into the line (say the line without "now" and you will hear it even more clearly). This pause dramatizes the reflective nature of the conjoined clauses as well as the time signature of the thought. The question begs itself: is "now" the present of the narrative or is "now" the constant present of the utterance? Do you *always* have no nation but the imagination?

In returning to that moment of crisis, Walcott pits language against praxis, and raises the hand of language as the victor. In doing so he wrestles with historians such as Franklin W. Knight, who claims in that "language, of course, has little relevance to political culture. Political, social, and economic patterns in the Caribbean seldom conform to the linguistic or cultural boundaries."[75] The pun is of course with the "nation" embedded within the word "imagination." Shabine attempts to empty "nation" of its significance by wedding it to "image."

The "image-in-nation," then, is a reflection of the very title of this section, "Shabine Leaves the Republic." While we can take this to mean that Shabine exits his inhabited place to begin an exodus, any familiarity with Walcott's work strongly invites a reader to recognize "leaves" as another well-placed Walcottian pun. He even puns "leaf" in the very body of this canto: "the Budget turns a new leaf." In fact, Walcott frequently turns objects of nature and the very landscape of his surroundings into metaphors of print, writing, and erasure. As much as it may signify that he abandons the Republic, "Shabine Leaves the Republic" means as much that Shabine *reads through* the republic, that he thumbs forward and backward through the pages of the Republic like a book, that he paints over the Republic as the swaying leaves mimic the strokes of a painter. "Archetypal dreams employ symbols of brokenness to depict the shedding of habit," wrote Wilson Harris. By "archetype" Harris means those signs that engage reality in challenging, creative discourse. "A naked jar sings in a hollow body, sings to be restored, re-filled with the

75   Franklin W. Knight, *The Caribbean: The Genesis of a Fragmented Nationalism* (New York: Oxford University Press, 1990), 314.

blood of the imagination. The jar sleeps yet sings." Harris's vision of symbolic language is one full of imagery and place—of landscape—through which all "haunting and necessary proportions of a new dialogue with reality in all its guises of recovered and revisionary tradition" encompass the inner workings of the re-emergent artist. "Inner ear and inner eye are [the] resurrected anatomy attuned to the music of painted silence in pulse and heart and mind arisen from the grave of the world."[76] Walcott's "Republic"—Shabine's patron of exile—is one of these "symbols of brokenness." To pun is to defamiliarize language from its standard context. It is, despite the external threat of banality through cliché, an othering of discourse. Hence, to defamiliarize language is also to slow it down, to ponder over it as its possible meanings well up, as though regarding one's vexing reflection in a dystrophic pool. Thus, the broken Republic is a crack in monumental language, revealing res ("thing") and publica (feminine of publicum, "public"). In its halted, fragmentary form the idea of the Republic is still a sign of remarkable power. For the unavoidable condition of the speaking exile is the burden to representation as the res publica or, in my butchered Latin, "the public thing."

Shabine is a poet—albeit a violently private one, though the intense protection of his poetry cannot quell the fact that his poetry becomes, in the end, public material. One of his shipmates steals Shabine's notebook, reads some of his poems, and mocks him. Shabine reacts quickly.

---

76   Wilson Harris, "The Music of Living Landscapes," *Selected Essays of Wilson Harris*, 42.

There wasn't much pain,
just plenty blood, and Vincie and me best friend,
but none of them go fuck with my poetry again.[77]

Whether fucked with again or not, his poetry has become a
shared text, an archetype of Caribbean creative expression and a
staple piece for its author. The chief crux of the poem is that the
character it portrays is in flux. Like the fragmented res publica,
"The Schooner *Flight*" portrays a consciousness in medias res:
any conclusions we come to based on the developing action we
therefore subject to serious questioning. While this by no means
implies that there is a true reading to a poem based on some con-
sideration of the present life of the poetic subject, there is much
to be gained from simply paying heed to the parts of a poem that
are in the past tense.

> Poetry, which is perfection's sweat but which must seem as
> fresh as the raindrops on a statue's brow, combines the nat-
> ural and the marmoreal: the past and the present, if the
> past is the sculpture and the present the beads of dew or
> rain on the forehead of the past. There is the buried lan-
> guage and there is the individual vocabulary, and the pro-
> cess of poetry is one of excavation and of self-discovery.[78]

This outlines what Walcott means by fragmented "epic mem-
ory." Walcott views the so-called buried language of the Carib-
bean as a starting point but not a resting point for self-discovery

---

77 Walcott, "The Schooner *Flight*," 355.
78 Derek Walcott, "The Antilles: Fragments of Epic Memory," *What the Twilight
Says: Essays* (New York: Farrar, Strauss and Giroux, 1998), 69–70.

of the individualized ars poetica. Poetry, as language, asks of others, and Walcott ends the poem with language imbued in an image that should produce in the end silence, yet metaphorically yields a fluid and incremental trope from which the process of creative imagining can begin again.

Shabine sang to you from the depths of the sea.

The poem's concluding conflation of death and poetry juxtaposes mystery to serialized information-gathering. Revelation is the slow matter of gathering and splitting words like fruit rather than the impetuous rash of discovery and reportage. Lest we forget that small "discovery" and "reportage" are what brought this predicament to the archipelago in the first place. As Glissant suggests, "Rather than discovering or telling about the world, it is a matter of producing an equivalent, which would be the Book, in which everything would be said, without anything being reported."[79] In contrast, Benedict Anderson saw novels and newspapers as producing a Benjaminian "homogenous, empty time . . . their fame . . . historical and their setting sociological." "This," he continues, "is why so many autobiographies begin with circumstances of parents and grandparents, for which the autobiographer can have only circumstantial, textual evidence; and why the biographer is at pains to record the calendrical, A.D. dates of two biographical events which his or her subject can never remember: birth-day and death-day."[80] Walcott displaces

---

79   Ibid.
80   Benedict Anderson, *Imagined Communities: Reflections on the Origin and Spread of Nationalism* (New York: Verso, 1991), 204.

birth-day and, as we may infer from the last line of the poem, death-day with the signs over which he pleads creative license. His, then, is not an autobiography in serial time but rather one within poetic time, full of its jumps, increments, and dwellings over fragmented objects, nation being one of them, but sound and word being of that mold as well. For Walcott, who recognizes exile as a useful point of departure into making art, the nation then remains distanced from the real world and can become for the poet parts to re-imagine with the imagination; republic can fracture into its Latinate flotsam and a patios slur for a name can become the "I" of a remembering consciousness ("I," which Walcott refers to as "that cry, / that terrible vowel"). The poetics of memory begin with memory's invocation of things and conspires with the imagination to shatter and re-arrange them. And yet, can this bring the res publica together? Through this gathering of broken pieces, which is Shabine's experience from Monos to Nassau, is a resounding yes. As it was as well for Walcott himself when he spoke upon receiving the Nobel Prize in Stockholm.

> Break a vase, and the love that reassembles the fragments is stronger than that love which took its symmetry for granted when it was whole. The glue that fits the pieces is the sealing of its original shape. It is such a love that reassembles our African and Asiatic fragments, the cracked heirlooms whose restoration shows its white scars. This gathering of broken pieces is the care and pain of the Antilles, and if the pieces are disparate, ill-fitting, they contain more pain than their original sculpture, those

icons and sacred vessels taken for granted in their ancestral places. Antillean art is this restoration of our shattered histories, our shards of vocabulary, our archipelago becoming a synonym for pieces broken off from the original continent.[81]

The nation—as an idea, as a principle, as a thing in and bestowed onto itself—need not be abandoned, though perhaps, in this English-language version of the Caribbean, we should split the trochee apart and re-fuse it. Perhaps we need not fly from the sign of the Republic but rather, fissured, speak of its aboriginal woe.

The possibility of nations is protected by the creative process of image-making by the victims of time and circumstance who, having been born instead of landed, struggle against the dominant eye that would have its surveyed be a "them" or worse yet an "it." Fanon reminds us of this crisis of interpretation:

> It must in any case be remembered that a colonized people is not only simply a dominated people. Under the German occupation the French remained men; under the French occupation, the Germans remained men. In Algeria there is not simply the domination but the decision to the letter not to occupy anything more than the sum total of the land. The Algerians, the veiled women, the palm trees, and the camels make up the landscape, the natural background to the human presence of the French.[82]

---

81   Walcott, "The Antilles: Fragments of Epic Memory," 69.
82   Fanon, *Wretched of the Earth*, 250.

The problem of interpretation placed before Shabine is to break imagination from nation while keeping the imagination intact. This has always been a Walcottian theme, since his most persistent metaphors have remained landscape and image as a metonym for writing. *Tiepolo's Hound* puts the theme for Walcott in its most explicit voice to date. In Walcott's nation of the image, a "lowering window resounds / over pages of earth, the canefield set in stanzas";[83] the "beach will remain empty / for more slate-coloured dawns / of lines the surf continually / erases with its sponge";[84] and in the Spanish Caribbean, the English-language poet might just "resist the return / of this brightening noun whose lines must be translated / into "el mar" or "la mar," and death itself to "la muerte."[85] But along with these metonyms of place is an anxiety over their constitution. Shoreline and its imprints, the colors of dawn, the indifferent return of the waves as las olas—these are images that test our faith in permanence. Yet will these images, these dividends of nation, return; and, even if they do will they be as they once were? This is the anxiety of a poetics of place that irks its desire to recall, recite, and retort (as opposed to a desire to report, which would be the sign of a cumbersome, as opposed to a creative, nationalism). A poetics of place in the Caribbean is the imagination's investment in a creative nation formed by a fractured, pictorial reality that faces up to its possible dissolution both in political and aesthetic form. Walcott is fundamentally a descriptive poet, and his poetics border a type of cyclical pictorialism. His is a manner of writerly

---

83   Derek Walcott, "I," *Midsummer* (New York: Farrar, Straus and Giroux, 1984).
84   Derek Walcott, "To Norline," *The Arkansas Testament* (London: Faber and Faber, 1988), 57.
85   Walcott, "XLIII," *Midsummer*.

reliance on visual phenomena—often evoked to describe writing itself—through images that are fraught with the inner workings of their inevitable erosion. Is either verse or vista permanent? Can they function as an artist's metaphor for freedom and imperishability, as both had (rhetorically at least) for so many of Walcott's English-language predecessors? The landscapes of the Caribbean region continually affirm and yet deceive. This implies a diurnal discord between dissolution/ruin and resuscitation/renewal that the poet sublimates through the anachronistic tenor of the trope ekphrasis. Since ekphrasis is the verbal representation of visual phenomena, it manifests an unavoidable problem: can writing or sound suitably reproduce what is seen, and why would we desire that either do so?

In his longer works *Another Life* and *Tiepolo's Hound*, Walcott writes within ekphrastic moments. In these works painting explicitly plays with and against the narrative thrust of the long poem. Passages such as the one below from chapter nine of *Another Life* insist on a relationship between self and landscape as being necessarily outside of time, like the close reading of poetry. They argue for a contentious, isochronal mode of recognition capable of significant change. Nation in Walcott's poetry is not only embedded within imagination but is also subject to the pun of I/eye, as well as to what "I/eye had."

> There are already, invisible on canvas,
> lines locking into outlines. The visible dissolves
> in a benign acid. The leaf
> insists on its oval echo, that wall
> breaks into a sweat, oil settles

in the twin pans of the eyes.
Blue, on the tip of the tongue,
and this cloud can go no further.
Over your shoulder the landscape
frowns at its image. A rigour
billows into the blue crowd,
A bird's cry tries to pierce
the thick silence of canvas.
From the reeds of your lashes, the wild commas
of crows are beginning to rise.[86]

The cyclical nature of Walcott's ekphrastic imagination ruptures other discourse—as verbal language and visual phenomena collapse—into a debate between the voice and the image. Which one is other? What does a "benign acid" do? Here creates an altered vision of the "muttering variegations of green." New vision, that which was already there yet invisible, still carries with it threat as ekphrastic fear builds.

At your feet
the dead cricket grows into a dragon,
the razor grass bristles resentment,
gnats are sawing the air,
the sun plates your back,
salt singes your eyes
and a crab, the brush in its pincer,
scrapes the white sand of canvass.
as the sea's huge eye stuns you

---

86   Walcott, "Another Life," *Collected Poems*, 197–98.

with the lumbering, oblique blow
of its weary, pelagic eyelid,
its jaw ruminates
on the seagrass it munches

What sustains in the face of this threat of loss (an anxiety-ridden one where landscape consumes landscape: in other words, subject consumes subject, nation consumes nation) is memory, the benefactor of the spatial still-time of the ekphrastic imagination. Memory, as an increment of recognition, makes failure if not tolerable, then survivable.

Remember, Vincent, saint
of all sunstroke, remember
Paul, their heads
plated with fire![87]

Shabine was a failed character who found nevertheless possibility from the fact that, as an artist, his failures might be mediated by what Benjamin would call "redemptive time," which would not redeem the individual in a moral sense but would re-create the effort, as is done by experiencing again a poem. In lyric time, however, there are few places of solace within a landscape as problematized as that of the Caribbean region for reasons we will probe further below. Nation as the articulation of ekphrastic hope is as tenable as a reach for the sun; the effort—imagine the gesture—further ostracizes the poet, and even in its possibility, it burns.

---

87 Ibid.

Dear Theo, I shall go mad.
Is that where it lies,
in the light of that leaf, the glint
of some gully, in a day
glinting with mica, in that rock
that shatters in slate,
in that flashing buckle of ocean?
The skull is sucked dry as a seed,
the landscape is finished.
The ants blacken it, signing.
Round the roar of an oven, the gnats
hiss their finical contradiction.
Nature is a fire,
through the door of this landscape
I have entered a furnace.[88]

Caribbean poets suffer a burden similar to that of African-American poets: the weight of an allegorical and capitalized self. The weight cleaved a schizophrenic poetics within Paul Lawrence Dunbar and has left camps of investors in Caribbean writers who place their stock in Walcott or dub poets as though either will pay.

In his search for suitable words for suitable images, Walcott risks an indictment worse than exile: uncommunicative, "indifferent" nature, more compelled by its "work" than by the challenge set to it by the artist who wishes to tame nature into landscape and landscape into nation.

I have toiled all of life for this failure.
Beyond this frame, deceptive, indifferent,

88   Ibid.

nature returns to its work,
behind the square of blue you have cut from that sky,
another life, real, indifferent, resumes.
Let the hole heal itself.
The window is shut.
The eyelids cool in the shade.
Nothing will show after this, nothing
except the frame which you carry in your sealed, sur-
   rendering eyes.

While the success of these poetic efforts are constantly subli-
mated by the absence of a resolute chord of completion, the
task it seems is left to forces exterior to the poem. The "sealed,
surrendering eyes" are what abates the onrush of ekphrastic in-
difference and fear. Akin to Shabine's diminuendo in the con-
cluding passage of "The Schooner *Flight*," "I stop talking now. I
work, then I read," one finds that both poems, despite crafting a
delicately aesthetic interior, cannot help but reference further, to
moments posterior to the poem. Ekphrasis, precisely because it
undulates space and time, fashions a way to capture an ulterior
purpose to poetics without sounding a prophecy. I would argue
that it is this very static, counternarrative reading encouraged
by ekphrasis that opens the borders for new national imaginings
and alternatives to incumbent political discourses.
   Walcott's work continually poeticizes the Caribbean's chief
export—its picturesque faux-exoticism—in its full (though per-
haps failing) splendor, remaining cognizant that it remains a site
of imminent and ruinous difficulty. For empires, and just as im-
portant for the idea of empire, the ruin as artifact is art-in-fact.

Empires hope to exploit the vague temporal links to antiquity that imagined ruins inspire.

Anne Janowitz writes that "in order to coerce its culturally complex populations into the industrial and globally imperialist age, 'Britain' calls upon the figure of ruin to secure its past." Yet, though the ruin as evoked by imperial Britain attempts to reify a sense of perpetuity onto its expanses it nevertheless "cannot help asserting the visible evidence of historical and imperial impermanence."[89] Ruin, captured by the national imagination of Britain at the same time that the museum was beginning to take a prominent role for captured artifacts and their reproductions, is an example of serialized time that cannot function convincingly in the Caribbean.[90] The tempting canonical possibilities of a doppelgänger Caribbean literary history are shelved invitingly for its writers—a perjurious shorthand—as Walcott intimates in his early "Ruins of a Great House."

> Stones only, the disjecta membra of this Great House,
> Whose moth-like girls are mixed with candledust,
> Remain to file the lizard's dragonish claws.
> The mouths of those gate cherubs shriek with stain;
> Axle and coach wheel silted under the muck
> Of cattle droppings.
> Three crows flap for the trees
> And settle, creaking the eucalyptus boughs.
> A smell of dead limes quickens in the nose

89 Anne Janowitz, *England's Ruins: Poetic Purpose and the National Landscape* (Cambridge, Mass: B. Blackwell, 1990), 4.
90 Jonah Siegel, *Desire and Excess: the Nineteenth-Century Culture of Art* (Princeton: Princeton University Press, 2000).

The leprosy of empire.

. . . . . .

A green lawn, Broken by low walls of stone,
Dipped to the rivulet, and pacing, I thought next
Of men like Hawkins, Walter Raleigh, Drake,
Ancestral murderers and poets, more perplexed
In memory now by every ulcerous crime.[91]

No, the imperial tropology of ruin will not do. Far from a continuation of national narrative, it is instead, in this region, a rut.

Marble like Greece, like Faulkner's South in stone,
Deciduous beauty prospered and is gone[92]

Appropriately, the blank page in search of something that will suffice may find that modern Caribbean poetry still has much use for its landscapes, no matter how vexing the proposition may appear. The prospects at times appear bleak for two overarching reasons: one being landscape's materialist presence as an export that rarely invests what it reaps within the foundations of an appropriately self-motivated infrastructure. The other reason involves the impulse of Caribbean artists to avoid national landscapes for fear of complying with and partaking of their own fetishization and the pastoral impressions of empire looking seaward.[93]

---

91 Walcott, "The Ruins of a Great House," *Collected Poems*, 19–20.

92 Ibid.

93 Paget Henry refers to these cruxes, respectively, as "historicist" and "poeticist" conditions of Caribbean thought. Cf., Paget Henry, *Caliban's Reason: An Introduction to Afro-Caribbean Philosophy* (New York: Routledge, 2000).

Much like the locus classicus of ekphrastic hope, the "Shield of Achilles" episode in Book XVIII of the *Iliad*, Walcott's descriptive moments are an interior and altering moment within a longer narrative. It is the narrative's flowering ulcer, slowing time down to descriptive subsets of human consciousness. It chooses visual space over narrative time. It obsessively calls attention to itself as difference and thus frames gaps though which necessary processes of change may take place. Ekphrasis is a quietly social trope that makes its need for a pragmatic audience, a community, implicit in its change of the image into word, the word into image. It asks of a community to imagine as opposed to being imagined, and to intelligently inhabit the fractured time therein. Even ensconced within a love poem like "To Norline," stacked squat like a typically low-lying home and the concluding poem in the "Here" section of *The Arkansas Testament*, the intent of the imagistic wish to redress time and memory beckons as a consideration of domestic and aesthetic borders.

To Norline

This beach will remain empty
for more slate-coloured dawns
of lines the surf continually
erases with its sponge,

and someone else will come
from the still-sleeping house,
a coffee mug warming his palm
as my body once cupped yours,

to memorize this passage,
of a salt-sipping tern,
like when some line on a page
is loved, and it's hard to turn.[94]

The page that is hard to turn either revels in its avid readership or suffers under the gaze of a somnolent one through which words begin to blur from fatigue or disinterestedness. Love in this instance is what clarifies the blur of the poem's scenery and intent. Yet love, as another ambiguity, seeks out a slow heterogeneous time. For it is this "someone else" that is left to memorize the poet's image ("this passage") "of a salt-tipping tern"—yet another portly pun—as the poem concludes with an analogy that also chafes against the need to "turn the page." This is the burden of the descriptive imagination as it faces its boundaries. It asks for a community that dares to slow down its ontological frames in order to draw and redraw, to address and redress, the parameters of the nation. "To Norline" reads, one can imagine, as one of the stolen poems within Shabine's book that he fought so vehemently to protect, as a "To Maria Concepcion." And though Caliban is now *le roi soleil* of Caribbean agency, there is still room within the growing archive for "nobody," that "someone else" who rises from the stanza to memorize the multiple meanings of "passage" along the ever erasing edges of the sea.

94   Walcott, "To Norline," 57.

I

Let's begin with a conclusion: Robert Hayden's sense of form
Was sporadic—beautifully so—and was set in motion less
By a cataloging of syllables and lines, but rather more

By the carnival of the idea: the mask the poet
Dons and unashamedly casts onto others (they can't help them-
    selves).
There are glimpses of his ideas regarding the Hopkins sonnet

In "Frederick Douglass" and of the persistence of the iambic
Pentameter line in "Middle Passage." Yet Hayden remains quite
    slippery:
It is difficult, if not impossible, to devise anything definite

And encompassing from Hayden on form. One reason for this
    inconsistency
Is that Hayden clearly saw the notion of form as rhetoric,
The thematic characteristics of any form being of equal priority

To the shape and texture of any poem. The project
Of being a formal poem, I believe, Hayden left alone
(One cannot thumb through *Collected Poems* and announce
    "formal poet").

The second reason for the formal ambiguities in Robert Hayden
Is sadly a matter of circumstance: due primarily to teaching,
His output, though marvelous, was hardly prolific. His *Collected
    Poems*

Reveals the heights of his powers; but those now seeking
To examine his experiments in form have only a few
Verses in any given style to wade in. Thus reaching

A conclusion regarding form in Hayden would be a coup
In and of itself. There are no staunch sequences here,
No book-length investment and subsequent disavowal: from
    form to chaos

And perhaps back again. What we do have are spare
Moments of form. One sonnet here, another, a Villon ballade,
Verse epistle, resonating through the volume like sound through
    air.

When a reader annuls the simoniac "Look what I've made"

(Meaning when a poem, pardoned from its pew, can cough)
There then is the passerby's fondness to find a shape

And to focus on its spirit. Take Hayden's ballads as
One example. There are three of them: "The Ballad of Sue
Ellen Westerfield," "A Ballad of Remembrance," and "The Ballad of

Nat Turner." They revel in their titles, yet barely use
The blueprint a ballad presumes. So self-conscious, then so loose.

II

The most recognizable ballad stanza fissures together two broken
    fourteeners
In a hymn meter, rhyming them *abcb*
Or *abab*; or some variation in-between them.

Times have lead to changes, some variations within the scheme;
But the idea has remained that one could both hear
A ballad's sonics and see it deployed on text clearly.

Yet "The Ballad of Sue Ellen Westerfield" for one appears
To heed the content-oriented nuances of the form, and prioritizes
These aspects as the vital components of the poem's sheer

Success as a ballad. Why is this a ballad, aside
From the fact that the poem's title urges it be?
When one looks at a poem like "Westerfield" one finds

The title siphoning the familiar music from the poem's body.
What comes from title to first line is the immediate
Withdrawal from the pattern. Line one, a surprise: an alexandrine.

She grew up in bedeviled southern wilderness
Then, the rest of the first stanza; with no hint
Of hymnody, nor of quatrains, no fourteeners, no matching
    assonance.

She grew up in bedeviled southern wilderness,
but she had not been a slave she said,
because her father wept and set her mother free.
She hardened in perilous rivertowns
and after The Surrender,
went as maid upon the tarnished Floating Palaces.
Rivermen reviled her for rankling cold
sardonic pride
that gave a knife-edge to her comeliness.

Though far from the stanzaic cobblestone expected of the ballad,
The poem is engaging heavily with a process of portraiture
Quite common to, and representative of, this particular form
    and

Its moods. The poem seeks to introduce, quickly, a character
Placed in circumstances beyond that individual's control, *in*
    medias res,
The unimportant material rushed through, a sense of the episodic,

The enforced narrative distance (Sue Ellen Westerfield was Rob-
    ert Hayden's
Mother), subverted by the hint—in "she said"—of interwoven
Discourse sublimated into one lyric poem. Note in another case—

"Those Winter Sundays" we find the poet's voice in tender
Mood and reflection, addressing the subject here as "my father."

III

Those Winter Sundays

Sundays too my father got up early
and put his clothes on in the blueblack cold,
then with cracked hands that ached
from labor in the weekday weather made
banked fires blaze. No one ever thanked him.

I'd wake and hear the cold splintering, breaking.
When the rooms were warm, he'd call,
and slowly I would rise and dress,
fearing the chronic angers of that house,

Speaking indifferently to him,
who had driven out the cold
and polished my good shoes as well.
What did I know, what did I know
of love's austere and lonely offices?

As in this sonnet, Hayden could have had easily written
"The Ballad of My Mother," or at the very least
Could have used her married name of Hayden. "Those Winter

Sundays" is, however, approaching its matter particularly as a
   lament.
This use of a more familiar diction exacerbates and canals
The questioning pose taken up poignantly in the poem's last

Lines. The sonnet is also deployed as a private channel,
Intoning the complicated domestic register by its placement of
   father
And then son in different stanzas, as in separate rooms.

Given the formal appropriateness of the sonnet as a factor
(Though to normalize the sonnet evoked as a love poem
between father and son is a luxury of the latter)

In its deployment by Hayden, we can then perhaps assume
That the ballad likewise owned particular inflections that made
   it
As seductive for what it signifies: a desirous, shoeless form.

Thus the form signifies a genre, a thematic pattern: naked,
Stripped of the identifiable syllables and spaces that the title
Makes such grand allusion toward. But is it all erased?

When she was old, her back still straight
her hair still glossy black,

she'd talk sometimes
of dangers lived through on the rivers.

The first two lines of this second stanza tease out
A fourteener, faithfully metrical. A phantasm of the form known,
Not heeded; "she'd talk sometimes" though not necessarily in
    meter.

Ballads memorialize the heroic, often tragic efforts of their
    constituents.
This is for Hayden the form's first idea, its architecture.

IV

In his considered nuances of technique Hayden separated from
    shape
What aspects of a form he wished to keep. Genre
Then may be more Hayden's sense of structure than is stanzaic

Pattern. A poem like "Night, Death, Mississippi" lets one ponder
Hayden's aesthetic of form from another angle. Given the oppor-
    tunity,
Without knowledge of their titles, to identify which of either

"Westerfield" or "Mississippi" was the ballad, many would likely
Pick the latter. It behaves as a ballad of false
Intuition. It dresses up like a loose one, so why

The discrepancy? Hayden's next ballad "A Ballad of Remembrance"
     fits
Into the discussion here because it too seems far removed
From the form, and also strays from the thematic fronts

Of the ballad that "Westerfield" highlighted with such purpose.
     "Remembrance"
Does not, cannot, fix on an individual at its start.
The bard is lost in a carnivalesque masque, unexpected penance

From which he is rescued by the familiarity of Mark Van Doren.

Then you arrived, meditative, ironic,
richly human; and your presence was shore where I rested
released from the hoodoo of that dance, where I spoke
with my true voice again.

And therefore this is not only a ballad of remembrance
for the down-South arcane city with death
in its jaws like gold teeth and archaic cusswords;
not only a token for the troubled generous friends
held in fists of that schizoid city like flowers,
but also, Mark Van Doren,
a poem of remembrance, a gift, a souvenir for you

There is something reminiscent of *Rime of the Ancient Mariner*
Here, though the bard (clearly Hayden) draws a vital distinction

Between "ballad" and "poem"—with "ballad" surfacing as an
     anodyne,

And as such containing some quality distinct from the "gift"
Hayden considers poetry to be. The ballad becomes necessary
form

And as such follows a patterning first and foremost pertinent
To the metrics of narrative. Hence, while these ballads contain
Repetitions, they function only as mimetic devices for the
personae

As opposed to a mnemonic device for a separate context:
A reader or some other audience, such as in "Westerfield."

How long how long was it they wandered,
loving fearing loving

V

I have saved for last "The Ballad of Nat Turner"
So as not to talk too much of it. So
We find here the discarded pattern, the alluded-to template.

Three ballads, three narrators, and it is in the cadences
Of the Black Jeremaid that we encounter the closest approximation
Of the traditional ballad form. It is important to consider

That the poem takes place before Turner's action and condemnation
And is another "ballad of remembrance" in its formal ambition
To pattern the ballad as something distinctive to the inducted.

Clearly, anonymity to Hayden was not of prime narrative impor-
    tance.
Neither was hymn meter (though Turner rightly comes closest).
Neither was rhyme. Yet as I peruse the sparse agreements

In each stanza—"far" and "fire," "amber" and "waver"
I keep returning to blackness and blackness, time and time.
Blackness with blackness, then time. From disinterested rhyme
    to obsessed.

There's the coda, the aesthetic moral: that something must lie
Between our carelessness and our mania, as Hayden well knew.

ROWAN RICARDO PHILLIPS's essays, poems, and translations have appeared in numerous publications. He is also the author of *The Ground* (2010). He has taught at Harvard, Columbia, and is currently Associate Professor of English and Director of the Poetry Center at Stony Brook University.

SELECTED DALKEY ARCHIVE PAPERBACKS

SELECTED DALKEY ARCHIVE PAPERBACKS

FOR A FULL LIST OF PUBLICATIONS, VISIT:
www.dalkeyarchive.com